sex and the city℠

KISS AND TELL

sex and the city℠

KISS AND TELL

WITH AN INTRODUCTION BY
sarah jessica parker

WRITTEN BY **AMY SOHN**
DESIGNED BY **NUMBER SEVENTEEN**

PRODUCED BY **MELCHER MEDIA**

First published 2002 by Pocket Books

First published in Great Britain 2002 by Channel 4 Books
an imprint of Pan Macmillan Ltd
20 New Wharf Road
London N1 9RR
Basingstoke and Oxford

Associated companies throughout the world
www.panmacmillan.com

07522 6505 9

1 3 5 7 9 8 6 4 2

A CIP catalogue record for this book
is available from the British Library.

This book was produced
by Melcher Media, Inc.

The pink Croco Pellaq
by Skivertex® cover material is
produced by FiberMark DSI.

Printed by The Bath Press, Bath

contents

Introduction

On Friday, March 27, 1997, I met a man named Darren Star who asked me to play the lead in the new HBO television series, *Sex and the City*. On Monday, June 2, only two and a half months later, I began filming the first day of what would become one of the great, if not greatest, professional experiences of my three decades as a working actor.

Some of the original elements of the show that first attracted me were the fresh voice of a very specific single woman in a very specific city; the candid, forthright, and intimate friendships of four women; the uniqueness and importance of these friendships; the heartbreaks, hopes, loneliness, and triumphs of being single; and the way in which we illustrate our love for our home, New York City. We have tried to remain true to these elements while continuing to grow and challenge ourselves to reflect the passing of years and the changes in our city.

Today, in late spring 2002, my feelings of affection, admiration, love, and respect for *Sex and the City*—the show, the extraordinarily talented writers, cast, and crew, the company I work for—only deepen, which seems impossible when my heart has been so full for so long.

But perhaps nobody has been more important than our viewers, whom we cherish and honor, those who were with us early on, as well as our most recent audience. We hope people will be able to read or look through this book and have a more full understanding of what the *Sex and the City* experience has been like for me and the whole *Sex and the City* crew. As I looked through pictures from seasons past and remembered stories from the set, I felt unbelievably proud to be a part of this show. But the thing I am most proud of is that you have been there with us. Because you are indeed truly a part of the *Sex and the City* family.

This book is for you.

love,

Sarah Jessica

IN THE BEGINNING

Once upon a time on a small island
not too far away,
there lived four smart,
beautiful women
who were all very good friends.

Carrie Bradshaw was a journalist who chronicled the battle of the sexes in her popular *New York Star* column, "Sex and the City." Charlotte York was an art dealer who felt the best way to get a man was to play by the rules, Samantha Jones was a public relations executive who believed women could have sex like men, and Miranda Hobbes was a corporate lawyer frustrated by the indignities of dating but reluctant to settle for less than she deserved. Two of the women were blondes, one

was a brunette, and one was a fiery redhead. But all four had one thing in common: none of them had found Mr. Right.

These women liked to eat, drink, date, and shop (one liked buying shoes so much she almost wound up penniless), but mainly they liked to *talk*. When it came to their love lives, it seemed they could never agree on anything. They debated a wide variety of hot topics: marriage, divorce, pregnancy, honesty, fidelity, compatibility, and **commitment**. They discussed favorite positions, strange new predilections, and the ever-popular "location, location, location." They yelled and even got into fights, but when push came to shove, they were always there for one another.

Sometimes it was hard to believe four such very different women could wind up friends in the first place. But they lived on the one shimmering island in this world where the strangest sorts of people have a way of coming together.

Where people get around in small yellow buggies, go to delis at four in the morning, drink big, pink cocktails, and run into exes when they least want to see them. A city of towering heels and nerves of steel, so bold and alive that no matter what day of the week it is, there's always a party somewhere. An island with so many single guys that you can find a "man" right inside its name. The island was called . . . **Manhattan.**

CHARLOTTE YORK
Art Dealer
Unmarried Woman

SAMANTHA JONES
Public Relations Executive
Unmarried Woman

MIRANDA HOBBES, ESQ.
Corporate Lawyer
Unmarried Woman

the pilot

Sex and the City began as a glint in the eye of Darren Star. In 1995 the prolific and savvy television producer, best known for creating *Melrose Place* and *Beverly Hills, 90210,* was making a new show for CBS, *Central Park West,* and living in New York City. He became a fan of a column called "Sex and the City," written by a Manhattan gal-about-town, Candace Bushnell, and published in the snarky pink weekly, the *New York Observer.*

The column chronicled the dating exploits of models, modelizers, bicycle boys, psychomoms, and toxic bachelors—mocking them for their narcissism in a smart, laconic style. Carrie Bradshaw was Bushnell's alter ego, and it was said that Carrie's on-again off-again boyfriend, Mr. Big, was modeled on then-*Vogue* publisher Ron Galotti.

After Bushnell interviewed Star for a magazine article in conjunction with the launch of *Central Park West,* the two became friends, and he began thinking about creating a television show based on "Sex and the City." What really got him, Star says, "was the idea of a single woman in her thirties writing about relationships and using that column as a tool of self-discovery about her own life, sometimes even unbeknownst to herself."

Having cut his teeth on drama, Star wanted to try his hand at a comedy, a comedy about sex from a female point of view, which was a totally uncharted arena on TV. He had some early discussions with ABC, but felt that the network couldn't fulfill what he had in mind. "They weren't even sure they could call it *Sex and the City,*" he recalls. In addition, he didn't like the way networks tended to handle adult sexuality: in a wink-wink, nudge-nudge style, euphemistic and adolescent. Instead he wanted to create a true adult comedy in which the sex could be handled in an up-front and honest way.

He didn't want it to be shot in the traditional sitcom format, with a live audience, a set, and four cameras. The show would be single-camera (like a film), similar to *Melrose Place,* with no audience and no laugh track. He knew that style would work well on HBO because it would be easily compatible with movies. "I wanted people to be able to watch the show and not feel like they were suddenly watching television," says Star. "I wanted it to bridge the gap between a television series and a movie." In the summer of 1996 he approached HBO with the idea. They embraced the concept immediately and gave him a deal to write and produce a pilot.

When Bushnell's column was published in book format in 1996, Star found his core characters: Miranda Hobbes, Samantha Jones, and Charlotte Ross (whose last name was changed to York for the show), all of whom were featured in the book. "At one point I was thinking it would be an anthology series," he says, "just Carrie and a different story every week. But when *Sex and the City* became a book, I decided to give her these friends and have her explore the issues with them."

He finished the pilot in January 1997 and hired Susan Seidelman (*Desperately Seeking Susan*) to direct. As for casting, the only actress he wanted to play Carrie was Sarah Jessica Parker, of whom he was a huge fan. "If you have an emotional character who has sex freely, is independent, and talks about sex, you have to find an actress who can make that character sympathetic," says Star. "I felt Sarah Jessica would bring a sense of romanticism and humanity to the character. I needed the combination of her and the role."

When Parker heard about the project, she was reluctant to sign on. "I hadn't done a television show in ten years," she says, "and was content doing movies and theater. My agent said, 'Normally I would discourage you from doing something like this, but there's something about this part. Read the pilot script and we'll talk about it afterwards.' "

She did and, intrigued by the final scene between Carrie and Big, agreed to have lunch with Darren Star, who offered to make her a producer if she signed on. "She's the kind of actress where as a writer you would feel really comfortable with her throwing in her two cents," Star says. "I felt it was important for her to be more than just the actor."

"He was very persuasive," Parker remembers. "He's a dog with a bone, which is why he's achieved so much." She showed the script to her husband, actor Matthew Broderick, and her brother, writer and director Pippin Parker, and asked for feedback. They told her she'd be foolish not to do it, so she signed on.

With Parker on board, Star and renowned New York casting directors Billy Hopkins, Suzanne Smith, and Kerry Barden and L.A. casting director Ellie Kanner assembled the rest of the cast. They cast Kristin Davis, with whom Star had worked on *Melrose Place*, as Charlotte; veteran New York theater and film actress Cynthia Nixon as Miranda; Willie Garson as Carrie's gay pal Stanford Blatch; Chris Noth as Mr. Big; and, finally, femme fatale Kim Cattrall as Samantha.

The pilot was shot in June, over ten days. The personalities of the four women were all visible—Samantha had an uninhibited, free-spirited approach to sex, Charlotte was a rosy-eyed idealist, Miranda was pithy and deadpan, and Carrie was inquisitive, smart, and yearning. The eyebrows were a little less tweezed, the lighting wasn't wonderful, and Carrie was a brunette, but the roots of the show were all there: the city, the dialogue, the sex, the friendship, and, most importantly, the chemistry.

"What you can see from the pilot," says Star, "and what Sarah Jessica brought, is the idea that here's a character who still hasn't given up on the idea of love. That romanticism is very much alive in this character. And the chemistry between Chris and Sarah was electric, which is why casting is so important. I could see the series in the pilot. That's when I thought, *We have a show here*."

> ## Star wanted to create a true adult comedy where the sex could be handled in an up-front, honest way.

"I'm missing the bride gene. I should be put in a test tube and studied."

—CARRIE BRADSHAW

CARRIE BRADSHAW

PLAYED BY SARAH JESSICA PARKER

"Writing Carrie is about opening up your heart and your head at the same time," says writer and executive producer Michael Patrick King. Carrie Bradshaw, gal-about-town and *New York Star* columnist, is the show's heart, head, and, quite literally, its voice. With her intelligence, loyalty, mind-boggling fashion sensibility, and open heart, she is the best friend every girl wants and the girlfriend every guy dreams of.

While audiences watch the show for everything from the heels to the comebacks to the come-ons, Carrie's search for a man while she struggles to maintain her independence has always been the show's central emotional story line. Unlike other television heroines, Carrie does not see marriage as the be-all and end-all of life. This tension—a longing for connection coupled with an innate instinct to stay her own course—is what makes her so intriguing to watch and her stories so intriguing to follow.

"Carrie is on a journey," says Sarah Jessica Parker, "whether she wants to admit it or not. She is looking for contentment. Whether that means she is alone in the end or with somebody or with a roommate, I don't know. But it is a recognizable journey."

Carrie has an uncompromising generosity of spirit. She dated a man who wanted to pee on her, yet gave the decision some serious thought. She went out with a bisexual guy and, instead of judging him, accompanied him to a party at which she was the only hetero. And in the most quintessential Carrie moment, she got into a cab with Natasha, the bleeding wife of the man she was having an affair with, to ensure she arrived safely at the hospital.

Much of Carrie's growth has come from her two serious relationships—with Big and with Aidan Shaw. With Big, Carrie was at her most extreme—belligerent, pained, sexy, naive, protective, worshipful, posturing, and real. When they said goodbye at the end of Season Four, after a carriage ride through Central Park, it was hard to imagine how she, or we, could ever live a Big-free life.

Aidan appealed to Carrie's more self-assertive instincts. A stable, down-home good guy, he forced her to examine her own commitmentphobia, her own Big-esque qualities. Aidan's patience and adoration seemed to soothe her restless spirit and enable her to grow with him. Yet after two attempts at a relationship—one that led to an affair and one that led to an engagement—Carrie remained conflicted, and Aidan left her. After four years, our heroine was once again alone.

While Carrie's relationships with men may be charged and difficult, her relationships with Charlotte, Miranda, and Samantha are always strong and vibrant. Though she gets into fights with them—over having an extramarital affair, her pattern with Big, even her choice to get engaged—each of the three women feels Carrie is her best friend. She is supportive, a good listener, and seldom judgmental, which enables them to confide in her in ways they might not confide in one another.

Carrie is a blithe spirit, smart, questioning, striving. She is always on the go, ever vital, and ever dynamic; and because she is so complex, not just any man will do. And so we root for her to find one who is just as special as she, a soul mate for the woman who is the soul of the show.

BIO: Parker has been working in film, television, and theater for nearly thirty years. Her film work includes *State and Main*, *'Til There Was You*, *Mars Attacks!*, *The First Wives Club*, *Miami Rhapsody*, *Ed Wood*, *Honeymoon in Vegas*, and *Footloose*. Her breakthrough role was SanDeE* in *L.A. Story*, opposite Steve Martin. Parker first garnered recognition in the popular CBS series *Square Pegs*, which still runs in syndication. Her stage work includes a successful six-month run in the Tony-nominated Broadway production of *Once Upon a Mattress*, as well as roles in *How to Succeed in Business Without Really Trying*, and A. R. Gurney's *Sylvia*. She also appeared on Broadway in the title role of *Annie*. Born in Nelsonville, Ohio, and raised in Cincinnati, she appeared in her first television special, *The Little Match Girl*, at age eight. She studied ballet with the Cincinnati Ballet and American Ballet Theater and voice with the Metropolitan Opera. She is the national ambassador for the U.S. Fund for UNICEF and was awarded the 1995 American Civil Liberties Union Award. For her role as Carrie Bradshaw, she has earned three Golden Globe awards, a SAG Award, and three Emmy nominations. She resides in New York City with her husband, actor Matthew Broderick.

Opposite in circle: Sarah Jessica with her brother Aaron
Diagonally above left: Sarah Jessica with her brothers and sisters
Rachel, Andrew, Toby, and Pippin

21

Sarah Jessica Parker

HATCHING A PLAN When I read the pilot script, I liked it very much. I had never seen a character like Carrie before in movies or television. But after we shot the pilot, I hatched a plan with my agent to get me out of the show. I was afraid I would be on a series for the rest of my life. Everyone told me to just stop panicking and calm down. But once I spent a little time working for HBO I never looked back. I didn't know when they said I could be a producer that I could get involved to the extent that I wanted. There was so much I didn't know in the beginning and so much that I've learned. It makes the experience entirely different to have a stake in it beyond being an actor for hire.

CARRIE'S CHARACTER Carrie does smoke and she does enjoy cocktails, but she's actually old-fashioned. If she weren't old-fashioned, she wouldn't be on this endless search. She would have already married or settled. I try to give Carrie a sense of historical context in terms of how she fits in and who she thinks she is. In the final episode of Season Four, when she tells Samantha she and Big are going out for "drinks, dinner, dancing—very 'old New York,'" she means an evening that is truly classic. She doesn't entirely fit into that world but she has that in her head as her final destination. Carrie's heading toward classic, whatever that means for her.

"Carrie is a very honest person. You can say a lot of things about her, but she has a moral compass."

It's a little bit of Holly Golightly, it's a little bit of the writers for the *New Yorker*. It's Edith Wharton, Evelyn Waugh, and F. Scott Fitzgerald. But Carrie is also a product of her time.

People make sweeping judgments of the show and say it's about four women looking for sex, and it's just not. Someone who only cared about sex would not have told her boyfriend she had had an affair. She would have said "I can get away with it." But it haunted her, and that says a lot about who she is.

ABSOLUTELY FABULOUS I trip a lot on the show. I actually try to trip as often as possible. Some directors won't let me do it. They don't have the Buster Keaton in them. But the truth is, Carrie is such a wreck of a person so much of the time, and her apartment is such a mess, that she *should* trip over shoe boxes because they are in the way. She wears these crazy high heels, runs around the city, is always late, and is not particularly organized. There are a lot of physical comedians I admire: Steve Martin; my husband; my brother Toby, who is one of the great comedians; and Jennifer Saunders, who plays Edina on *Absolutely Fabulous*. I can't believe some of the stuff she does. It's so old-fashioned, broad, and hilarious. I've never seen somebody fall so much. The people on *Absolutely Fabulous* are really in my head when I do my work. I want to be as good as they are.

THE PRODUCER My role as producer has changed dramatically over the years. In the beginning, luckily I had the presence of mind not to open my mouth when I didn't know anything. I contributed when I felt I was useful, but I also shut up, listened, and learned. I felt that the most I could contribute was the fact that I was a real New Yorker. I was the only producer on the show who had spent time here since I was a young child, so I felt I needed to speak for the city.

"I felt responsible to this city and protective of its image." **–SARAH JESSICA PARKER**

I also wanted the women to look a certain way. I worked very hard on preparing the makeup to ensure that no base would be used. Women in New York do not wear complete makeup. We have a rule in the makeup and hair trailer that if you can't do it, you can't do it. If I can't do what's going to be done to my hair, unless it's a special event and I would have gone to a beauty parlor, then I won't do it on the show.

I was also concerned about language and choice of words. Carrie's a writer, and I didn't think it was a good idea for her to use a lot of profanity. I thought she should be thoughtful about her words and try to be as articulate as possible. Just because we can show women and men nude, use bad language, and be ribald and salty doesn't mean we always should. I knew the show could not be about four women going around using bad language and sleeping with a lot of men. The novelty of that would last about twenty minutes.

Over time my role as producer has become more involved. I'm either in a meeting or a fitting, doing narration, doing an interview, looking at the marketing, auditioning actors, reading rewrites, looking at a daily, talking about directors, or meeting a director. The thing that's hardest about my responsibilities is I can't hang out with the crew as much as I used to.

GIRL TALK I love the women. They do an amazing job. I think they're extraordinary, and in a million years I could not see anyone else playing those parts.

The coffee-shop scenes are hard for us because they are so long. But it's also when we laugh the most. It will be the twelfth hour you have been working, saying those freaking lines, and the camera is finally on you, and suddenly you do not remember your lines anymore. The minute the camera is on you, you are fried. We could do reels of outtakes of us in those scenes laughing our asses off, not knowing what's going on, not knowing the lines, not knowing what the topic is.

I'M NOT ME AND YOU ARE NOT YOU Big and Aidan are ideal men to tell the story of Carrie and her relationships with men. Chris Noth and John Corbett have been willing to be "types" to be projected upon. There were times when it was frustrating for John. He would say, "Why are they breaking us up? I don't want to say that to you," and I'd say, "I don't want to do this, but we have to." Chris struggled for a long time with "I'm not this guy. This guy is so aloof." And I would say, "Keep doing it. Don't make him different than he's meant to be. It's good for the show, it's good for you, it's good for me, and it's good for the characters. I'm not me, and you are not you." You can't abandon your characters midship. You have to stick with it.

John is very funny, weird, and incredibly tactile. And Chris has done a great job of taking a very specific archetype of a man and forcing Big to be human. He's done a very good job of keeping the myth of Big but also explaining himself without using too many words, and he's done a good job of loving Carrie, caring about her.

THE WOMEN'S MOVEMENT These characters, and the actresses playing them, reap enormous benefits from the women's movement. The characters have sexual freedom, opportunity, and the ability to be successful. They have the ability to be leaders and to be strong, assertive, and confident. If you grow up with the right to choose, vote, dress how you want, sleep with who you want, and have the kind of friendships you want, those things are the fabric of who you are. But I don't think of it as a feminist show, because true feminists may take issue with certain things about the women and would want things to be different for them. Cleverly or not, we have steered clear of labeling ourselves, but that's also reflective of who we are as women.

Carrie's quandaries

Since birth, modern women have been told we can do and be anything we want. Be an astronaut, the head of an Internet company, a stay-at-home mom. There aren't any rules anymore, and the choices are endless. And apparently they can all be delivered right to your door. But is it possible that we've gotten so spoiled by choices that we've become unable to make one?

Does a string of bad dates really equal one good one? And will treating someone badly in one relationship ensure that you'll be treated badly in the next? Does everything that goes around really come around? And if so, will it come around to bite you in the ass?

Maybe you can't change a man, but once in a blue moon, you can change a woman.

In a city of infinite options, sometimes there's no better feeling than knowing you only have one.

"Soul mate." Two little words. One big concept. A belief that someone, somewhere, is holding the key to your heart and your dream house. All you have to do is find them. So where is this person? And if you love someone and it didn't work out, does that mean they weren't your soul mate?

What if Prince Charming had never showed up? Would Snow White have slept in that glass coffin forever? Or would she have eventually woken up, spit out the apple, gotten a job, a health-care package, and a baby from her local neighborhood sperm bank? I couldn't help but wonder: inside every confident, driven single woman, is there a delicate, fragile princess just waiting to be saved?

When *Sex and the City* premiered in June 1998, audiences knew they were witnessing television history.

In the very first ensemble scene, the women gathered at Lucky Cheng's for Miranda's birthday party and talked about sex with no holds barred. The question they debated was one that single people had been debating in their own social circles: "Can women have sex like men?"

Samantha argued that instead of trying to find long-lasting relationships, women should "just go out and have sex like a man . . . without feeling." Miranda noted that men "don't want to be in a relationship with you, but as soon as you only want them for sex, they don't like it." Charlotte refused to "give up on love," and Carrie asked, "Are we really that cynical? What about romance?" The roles were defined, the dialogue urbane and au courant; all the elements were in place.

In subsequent episodes the women dished about dozens of hotbed topics: blow jobs, threesomes, twenty-somethings, anal sex, secret sex, and why vibrators are better than men. Carrie received a thousand dollars after a hot night with an architect; Charlotte met a guy on Prozac who didn't care about sex; Miranda dated a modelizer; and Samantha ventured into tantric celibacy. Carrie and Mr. Big did the dance of intimacy: she nailed him on his tendency to look at other women, learned that he had been married before, and finally refused to go to St. Barth's with him, realizing she deserved someone who knew she was "the one."

Sex and the City's deconstruction of sexual and social conventions, mixed with a healthy dose of screwball comedy, seduced us from the beginning. Over the course of the season, the costumes grew more freewheeling, and the city a more vibrant participant in the drama. Carrie's up-and-down relationship with Mr. Big kept us hooked week after week, as Samantha's bedroom farces got more uproarious, Charlotte grew more sympathetic in her desire to meet Mr. Right, and Miranda exposed her touchstone combination of cynicism and vulnerability. In that formative and riotous first season, *Sex and the City* dug in its Manolo Blahnik heels for good.

THE FIRST SEASON *

*where one girl gets big, but feels small, another meets too small, and the show starts to hit it big

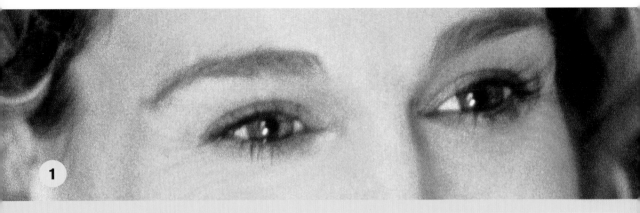

SEX AND THE CITY

WRITTEN BY *darren star*
DIRECTED BY *susan seidelman*

"Can women have sex like men?"
New York Star columnist Carrie Bradshaw tries to determine with her friends Miranda, Samantha, and Charlotte whether women, like men, can have sex without feelings. As an experiment, Carrie one-ups old flame Kurt Harrington, then meets Mr. Big; Miranda meets a young pushover, Skipper; Samantha has a one-night stand with Capote Duncan, a man Charlotte wouldn't sleep with on the first date.

SARAH JESSICA PARKER (CARRIE):

What the pilot did best was that moment when Big gives Carrie the ride home, and after that glib, surface conversation in the car says, "I get it. You've never been in love." And she makes some glib, sassy remark, and there's the "absofuckinglutely" moment, and then they freeze frame on her. I just thought, *Wow. This could go on forever. This person has a million stories to tell, and if she lived anywhere else this might not be the case. And who is this man? And why are they so exciting together?*

CHRIS NOTH (MR. BIG):

I didn't know Sarah Jessica at all when we shot that scene in the limo. I look at the distance between that and now, and it's very interesting to see how far we and the show have come. We didn't know what the show was, and slowly, to the beat of the drum, it started to create this roar. Sometimes we look at each other and say, "Can you believe this?"

MODELS AND MORTALS

WRITTEN BY *darren star*
DIRECTED BY *alison maclean*

"If models could cause otherwise rational individuals to crumble in their presence, exactly how powerful is beauty?"
Miranda makes the mistake of going out with a "modelizer" (someone obsessed with models); Samantha dates a voyeuristic modelizer who likes to videotape women he sleeps with; Carrie goes home with Stanford's new client, Derek the Underwear Model.

WILLIE GARSON (STANFORD):

This episode was the first time we'd done a fashion show. It was late, about one o'clock in the morning, and Candace Bushnell stopped by and said, "I want to be in it. I'm going to sit next to Stanford." We were trying to explain to her that if she sat down, she would be there for the next five hours; that it's not just this one shot. So they talked her out of it. It's so interesting to remember that fashion show and compare it to the one in Season Four, when we had a huge budget. It felt really great the first season because we didn't know. We just didn't know.

STANFORD: *How could you?* CARRIE: *I didn't. We just talked.* STANFORD: *I knew he was gay.*

3

BAY OF MARRIED PIGS
WRITTEN BY *michael patrick king*
DIRECTED BY *nicole holofcener*

"Is there a secret cold war between marrieds and singles?"

Carrie dates "Marrying Guy," that rare Manhattan man whose sights are set on marriage; Miranda pretends to be a lesbian to help her career; Samantha gets drunk at a "marrieds" party and winds up in bed with Charlotte's doorman; Charlotte dates Carrie's Marrying Guy but dumps him for liking the wrong china.

DARREN STAR (CREATOR):

There's a point at the end of this episode where, after the girls have gone on their separate adventures, they meet up at a movie theater and walk in with their arms around each other. There was a believable sense of warmth and camaraderie that allowed us to go to the more outrageous extremes. No matter what kind of adventures these girls go on, they are able to come back to the group, re-collect themselves, and touch base.

4

VALLEY OF THE 20-SOMETHING GUYS
WRITTEN BY *michael patrick king*
DIRECTED BY *alison maclean*

"Are men in their twenties the new designer drug?"

Carrie dates a twenty-something hunk as she tries to determine why a certain forty-something man is so complicated; Charlotte fears becoming Mrs. Up the Butt; Samantha gets rid of her boy toy when he notices the wrinkles in her neck; Miranda tolerates Skipper.

DARREN STAR:

I knew HBO would be great when I went in there and pitched them our first season. I said, "Charlotte's dating a guy who wants to have anal sex, and she doesn't want to become Mrs. Up the Butt." I thought, [HBO Original Programming president] *Chris Albrecht is either going to laugh or throw me out of the office.* And he laughed.

SARAH JESSICA PARKER:

This was one of the perfect episodes of all time. It had the anal sex discussion, Carrie seeing Big, Carrie going home with the twenty-something, walking down the street shopping, seeing Big in front of the Stanhope, Big running after her, them talking, her being in control, and then saying, "It would have been so cool if I hadn't looked back." From start to finish, it's a great episode.

MIRANDA: *If he goes up your butt, will he respect you more or respect you less? That's the issue.* DRIVER (TO CARRIE): *No smoking in the cab.*
CARRIE: *Sir, we're talking up the butt. A cigarette is in order.* SAMANTHA: *Front, back, who cares? A hole is a hole.* MIRANDA: *Can I quote you?*
SAMANTHA: *Don't be so judgmental. You could use a little back door.* CHARLOTTE: *I am not a hole.* CARRIE: *Honey, we know.*

29

5

THE POWER OF FEMALE SEX

STORY BY *jenji kohan*
TELEPLAY BY *darren star*
DIRECTED BY *susan seidelman*

"Where is the line between professional girlfriend and just plain professional?"

Carrie dates a French architect who leaves her a thousand dollars after they sleep together; a famous painter asks Charlotte if he can paint her unmentionable; Skipper goes *Fatal Attraction* on Miranda.

JEREMY CONWAY (PRODUCTION DESIGNER):

The vagina paintings embarrassed a lot of people. Two artists painted them for us, and one day I called an art director who works with me often, Kim Jennings, and said, "I've got these paintings we are doing for an upcoming show. They are large format and in four different styles, and I need you to come over and tell me if they are working in terms of color theory." When she walked into the studio and saw them, she got beet red, turned around, and left. And this is a Bennington girl!

6

SECRET SEX

WRITTEN BY *darren star*
DIRECTED BY *michael fields*

"How many of us out there are having sex with people we are ashamed to introduce to our friends?"

Carrie sleeps with Mr. Big for the first time and then worries he's secretly ashamed of her; Miranda meets a man who has a spanking fetish; Samantha realizes she has no secrets when it comes to sex; Charlotte reveals her past love affair with a Hasidic hottie.

MICHAEL PATRICK KING (EXECUTIVE PRODUCER):

There's a really bizarre scene in this episode when Carrie and Miranda are walking in Riverside Park. There is not a leaf on any of the trees, and they are wearing scarves. That was before we realized the actresses are going to be cold. From then on we decided the show would take place in a season called "Eternal Spring." It's never summer, fall, or winter until the final episode of Season Four.

SAMANTHA: *A guy could just as easily dump you if you fuck him on the first date as he can if you wait until the tenth.*
MIRANDA: *When have you ever been on a tenth date?*

30

7

THE MONOGAMISTS

WRITTEN AND DIRECTED BY *darren star*

"In a city like New York, with infinite possibilities, has monogamy become too much to expect?"

Carrie learns that Mr. Big is dating other women and decides she wants a monogamous relationship; Samantha two-times her realtor; Miranda's feelings for Skipper intensify when she sees him with another woman; Charlotte reveals that she doesn't like giving blow jobs, but no one is shocked.

DARREN STAR:

In this episode Charlotte dates a guy who has a dog. He wants a blow job from her, but she says no. She tells him she can't believe he's throwing the whole relationship away for a blow job and walks out. Originally when we shot it, she has a change of heart and walks back in to find that his golden retriever is going down on him. The actor had a tennis ball between his legs and the dog was trying to get it, bobbing up and down. That was too disturbing for HBO, so we cut it.

8

THREE'S A CROWD

WRITTEN BY *jenny bicks*
DIRECTED BY *nicole holofcener*

"Are threesomes the new sexual frontier?"

Carrie discovers that Mr. Big was once married, and that he and his ex participated in a threesome; Charlotte's boyfriend is mad about *ménage*; Miranda is devastated to learn that none of the girls would choose her for a hypothetical threesome; Samantha unwittingly gets too involved with a married man and his wife.

KEN (ON PHONE): *It's over. I told my wife.* SAMANTHA: *Who is this?*

31

MIRANDA: *You haven't met the Rabbit.* SAMANTHA: *Oh, come on. If you're going to get a vibrator, at least get one called the Horse.*

9

THE TURTLE AND THE HARE

WRITTEN BY *nicole avril & susan kolinsky*
DIRECTED BY *michael fields*

"In a city of great expectations, is it time to settle for what you can get?"

Mr. Big tells Carrie he will never marry again; after getting left out in the cold by a guy she met at a wedding, Samantha dates a guy named "The Turtle" and tries to turn him into a fox; Miranda introduces Charlotte to a vibrator called "The Rabbit," which turns Charlotte into a recluse.

DARREN STAR:

When we were casting this episode, we just could not find the right Turtle. When I saw the guy we cast on the set after he came out of hair and makeup, I said, "He's just too cute to be the Turtle." The scene was supposed to shoot in an hour. So we released him and called this other actor who had auditioned and who, for whatever reason, we hadn't hired. Thank God he was home. That was a nail-biting moment.

WILLIE GARSON:

In the scene where Stanford and Carrie are supposed to be leaving the ballet at Lincoln Center, they couldn't hire that many extras. So we waited till ten o'clock when they had a play, the ballet, and an opera letting out at once. We had one chance to get the shot, and we did. We're walking and talking, and there are literally ten thousand people exiting Lincoln Center behind us.

10

THE BABY SHOWER

WRITTEN BY *terri minsky*
DIRECTED BY *susan seidelman*

"Is motherhood a cult?"

The girls go to a baby shower for their old friend Laney. Carrie is late with her period but unsure whether she wants her pregnancy test to be positive or negative; Charlotte learns that Laney has stolen her prized secret baby name; and Laney yearns for her single days.

CINDY CHUPACK (CO-EXECUTIVE PRODUCER):

Before I worked on *Sex and the City* I wrote for *Everybody Loves Raymond*. One day one of the writers brought in a tape of this episode. We were all sitting around the conference table, and as we watched, one by one, all the men in the room got bored and went to lunch. I was left sitting there, and I was crying by the end. I was so moved by how honest and complicated it was. Soon after that I contacted Darren Star and told him how much I liked the show, and that I would love to do an episode.

KIM CATTRALL (SAMANTHA):

The scene where all of us appear in black and go to the baby shower was to me the beginning of us forming as a group of actors, as characters, with the writers. We all fell into it without trying to make it happen. It's a wonderful place to be because you're not breathing from your upper chest, you're breathing from your diaphragm.

MIRANDA: *You farted. You're human.* **CARRIE:** *I don't want him to know that.*

THE DROUGHT

WRITTEN BY *michael green & michael patrick king*
DIRECTED BY *matthew harrison*

"How often is normal?"

An accidental fart convinces Carrie she and Mr. Big will never share a bed again; Miranda is convinced she will never share a bed with any man again; Samantha forays into tantric celibacy with her yoga instructor before deciding abstinence is not in her best interest; Charlotte meets a guy on antidepressants who is happy not to have sex.

SARAH JESSICA PARKER:

When Michael Patrick King pitched me the story about Carrie farting in bed, I was so embarrassed, I didn't want to do it. Then I went and told my agent the story, and she was laughing so hard that I thought, *I'll do it.* When I was covered up with the blanket, I accidentally ran into the door, but we kept the shot. There was a lot of politicking for who was going to make the actual sound, and it ended up being Joe Dolly—his name is Joe Donohue, but I call him Joe Dolly. He is a third- or fourth-generation dolly grip and an incredibly bright, amazing young man. The scene took many takes because I kept laughing and I was really embarrassed.

OH COME ALL YE FAITHFUL

WRITTEN BY *michael patrick king* DIRECTED BY *matthew harrison*

"Are relationships the religion of the nineties?"

Carrie breaks up with Mr. Big, deciding to have faith in herself; Miranda breaks up with Catholic Guy, who must shower after sex; Samantha falls in love with James, a perfect man except for one small thing; every fortune-teller in the city tells Charlotte she will never marry.

KIM CATTRALL:

Michael Patrick King took the story line of Samantha meeting James at a jazz club from my life. My husband, Mark, and I met at a jazz club, and almost verbatim what we said to each other that night is in the scene. The unfortunate thing—or the fortunate thing—is that comedy is based on conflict. The conflict, of course, was that James was terrific in so many ways, but in bed he wasn't. When we shot the scene where Samantha says, "His dick is like a gherkin!" the boom man laughed so hard he dropped the boom. He was so apologetic. He said, "In my thirty-odd years of doing this, I have never ruined a take." I thought that was the greatest compliment, that this hard-bitten crew member was really enjoying what we were doing.

CHARLOTTE: *Is he a good kisser?* **SAMANTHA:** *Oh, who the fuck cares? His dick is like a gherkin.*

Although the final episodes are shaped by hundreds of people, it is the writers who give birth to the stories that comprise each episode. *Sex and the City*'s writing staff is small by network standards, but made up of some of TV's brightest writing talents. For the first three seasons, creator Darren Star was executive producer, or "show runner," in charge of the staff. Michael Patrick King, who first joined the show as a writer and co-executive producer in the first season, has been an executive producer since Season Two, and has been running the show since the fourth season, while Star has stayed on as executive consultant. The core writing group has, at one time or another, consisted of Cindy Chupack, Jenny Bicks, Allan Heinberg, writing duo Julie Rottenberg and Elisa Zuritsky, and Amy B. Harris.

How does such a small team pack so much punch into every episode? In the fall, four months before the show begins shooting, the writers gather in the show's Los Angeles offices to begin breaking the stories. They sit around a table coming up with the questions that Carrie asks in her column, and using those questions as triggers for the themes and plotlines. "Everything you see pretty much comes from the emotional life of one of us," says King. "For a month, all we do is talk about our lives, and then we put it all on the writers' board, and it forms the season."

"We'll talk about what we're sensing is out there," says Chupack, "where the characters have been in the last few seasons, and where we think their relationships should go." When they have enough meaty, entertaining story ideas, says Star, "we figure out how we can match the stories up in a relevant, entertaining, and surprising way."

In late November, when the writers have a basic idea of the plotlines for the season, the executive producer meets with Sarah Jessica Parker, also an executive producer, and pitches her the season. She asks pertinent questions and then notes whether she

> *Ask almost anyone why Sex and the City is a success, and you'll hear, "the writing."*

feels a plotline is one that has been used on the show. "I've never questioned the writers' instincts," says Parker. "I've been nervous about the direction they'll take something, but never their instincts."

> *Darren Star, Michael Patrick King, Cindy Chupack, and Jenny Bicks are* Sex and the City's *other fabulous four.*

The executive producer then assigns the first six to eight episodes. He'll do this with an eye toward who has the most "heat," or passion about a given story. "In 'Change of a Dress,'" recalls Chupack, "Carrie gets cold feet about getting married to Aidan. One of the writers on that story was someone who has been in a pretty long-term relationship and felt that way about weddings and marriage. If there's a writer who feels close to the emotional core of a story, then we will put that writer on it."

Eventually, detailed outlines and then scripts are presented to the executives at HBO Original Programming for comments and approval. According to Amy Harris, "They might say a certain story line isn't quite working, or that we don't have enough drive for that character, or something like 'Samantha would say that line instead of Carrie.'"

After the first group of episodes is written, usually by late February, the staff moves to New York and the show starts filming. This is when things get hectic. While the first group is in production, the writers work on the remaining episodes. Often they are influenced by the actors' work and way of interacting. For example, during Season Two, Steve and Miranda were set to last only three episodes. But when David Eigenberg was cast and the writers saw the chemistry between him and Cynthia Nixon, they decided to bring him back—twice. "When we see the first episodes being shot," says Chupack, "we can figure out what we're tired of and what we want to see more of."

With their wit and imagination, the writers are individual visionaries and a collectively ingenious team that make the show shine week after week.

DARREN STAR
CREATOR AND EXECUTIVE PRODUCER

EXPECTATIONS This show has always had a really easy process, as far as I'm concerned. It's one of those things that has always gone swimmingly. We shot the whole first season in the summer before a single episode aired, so we weren't responding to ratings, anybody's reaction, or critics. I always thought the show was funny. When we wrapped the season, I said to Sarah Jessica Parker, "You know, no matter what happens, we did something really special here."

I was at the point where I just had a show that really didn't work, *Central Park West,* and I thought, *Wow. This is either going to be the beginning or the end of my career.* That's what happens when you do something different. You get a little nervous.

After the first season had aired, and I wasn't sure if people were watching it, I was walking my dog up Runyon Canyon in Los Angeles and I heard people discussing the "Rabbit" episode. I thought it was a great sign to hear people talking about it.

SETTING THE MOLD In thinking about the concept for the title sequence, I looked at the openings to *The Mary Tyler Moore Show* and *That Girl,* which both tell a story about the character. We had just shot "Secret Sex," where Carrie's picture was on the side of a bus, and we had the bus available to us. So I came up with the idea that she would be walking in a confident, cocky way through the streets, this bus would splash her, and then she would turn around and see that it was her image. The show is about someone who is constantly getting surprised by life, and I felt the sequence encapsulated what the show was and who Carrie was.

> Before creating *Sex and the City,* Star executive-produced *Beverly Hills, 90210,* one of the longest-running prime-time series in television history, *Melrose Place,* and *Central Park West.* "20-Something Girls vs. 30-Something Women" is one of the many critically acclaimed episodes he has written and directed.

I put together the cast, the production team, the writers, and ran the show the first three seasons, which included everything from breaking the stories to supervising the scripts to editing, casting, sound mixing, to occasional directing.

You know you have done your job successfully as a show creator and runner if you have put a team together where one show is indistinguishable from the next. At a certain point I almost have to kick myself upstairs. It's my job to create and set the mold and to bring people on who can create shows in that mold week after week, year after year.

THE PLAYBOY CHANNEL On *Sex and the City,* you've got a group of characters who live in a world that the audience participates in vicariously. There's a sense that the characters are intimate and care about each other. Every episode has a strong story line with a beginning, middle, and end. One thing that was important to me when I was pitching the show, and was also important to HBO, was that it would not be a show about a lot of T&A. You can look at the Playboy channel anytime and see all the sex you want. People are never going to watch the show to get horny. They watch because it's funny. We are able to

do things that are as outrageous and explicit as they are because they're funny.

IT'S OKAY TO BE SINGLE People watch the show and think, *Yeah, that's me. That's my situation.* I think that the show has empowered a lot of people. It's a lot easier to get married when you feel like you are okay with yourself, and when you know you'd be okay on your own. By the time you get to your thirties, you have a sense of your own identity, and you know that identity should not have to be dependent upon another person, or on being married.

I don't believe that you could find four single men in their thirties as happy and independent as four single women in their thirties. It would be a depressing show. The women on the show are like a lot of women today who didn't feel a societal pressure to get married; they focused on their careers. So their journey has been more about self-discovery and personal empowerment than anything else. If they got married, great, and if they didn't, fine. One of the big messages of the show is that it is okay for a woman to be single.

MICHAEL PATRICK KING
EXECUTIVE PRODUCER

THE BEGINNING The first season it was just Darren and me doing the writing. We did twelve episodes. Jenny Bicks came in and did one episode and did great. Over the course of those first twelve episodes, we went up and down. What we eventually found was the beginning of the sense of humor and, I think, Carrie. In essence all the characters were there, but every year we've deepened the idea of who they are.

WRITING VERSUS DIRECTING The nightmare of directing our show is that it's very hard to join a show that's already a clique. The writers and actors know where we're going as a group, as a show, as an idea, and we know where we've been. In movies the director is God, the actors come second, and the writers come fifth. In our television show, which is shot like a movie, it's the writers, then the actors, and then the directors. The actors are very open and willing to listen. If Sarah Jessica is getting direction from a director that isn't working for her she will just look at me, the way a player does with a third-base coach. But when somebody comes in who is brilliant, it's a blast for us.

Directing my own stuff is the most fun because I already see and hear it while I'm writing, so it's just a matter of letting the actors bring it to life and making sure I have every comedic or emotional beat that I want. I've also directed Darren's stuff, which is really interesting because Darren writes completely differently than I do. He doesn't plot out the movement in his head as he's writing. For example, his scripts will read, "She enters the room" and later, "She is on the other side." I would think, *How do I get her there?* Darren would say, "You're the director. Find out."

THE FOUR SEASONS The show has grown like a relationship. The first season was the first date. You really didn't know the people. You were just watching them and noticing what they had on, and you were a little scared. The second season was like starting to date a couple times. You got a little bit more familiar and started to see stuff you didn't like. You enjoyed the sense of humor, you saw where they live, and you met their friends.

The third season was about that six-months-in point in a relationship where you start to see the flaws and all the "stuff" starts to come up. The risks of the third season were, now you're really in it and you're naked. The fourth season was about growing up and realizing that relationships are complicated and that even within them, you still have to take care of yourself. It is not about the other person, it's about you, and deciding whether you want to stay or not.

SEX AND THE EMERALD CITY In *The Wizard of Oz,* when the group leaves Munchkinland, they go to this drop that looks like the Emerald City, and when it's shown on TV, they always cut to a commercial at that point because the actors can't go through that drop. I feel that's what most television writing is like. You can feel writers saying, "That is as far as we can go. Cut to a commercial." They can't say the word they want to say. The girl can't have the affair with the married man because she's the good girl. But on our show she can.

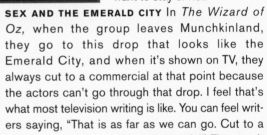

The Emmy-nominated second-season finale, "Ex and the City," and the moving fourth-season finale, "I Heart NY," are just some of the many episodes King has written and directed. Before joining the show, King was the co-executive producer on *Murphy Brown* and *Cybill*, and a consulting producer for *Will & Grace.*

It's pretty shocking the way Carrie messes up her life over and over again, between the cheating, the smoking, the losing the dog, and the lying. The idea of failing and loving yourself is a big thing in my own life—when something fails, learning to be okay with it and honoring what you tried to do. Carrie and Big's nobility, even when they don't get along, is something that I strive for.

I see *Sex and the City* as a human show. We get to say what no one would ever say to single people in their thirties, which is "Maybe your life is better than the married people's. Maybe." But we also try to show flaws in the single people, the flaws in the married people, as well as the love of the married people.

CINDY CHUPACK
CO-EXECUTIVE PRODUCER

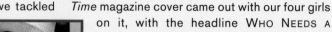

NO SOAP ADS In the fourth season we tackled some really big issues, such as death, abortion, testicular cancer, infertility, and divorce, and I feel like we've earned that right. The characters have evolved to the point where they can handle weighty topics with humor and grace. It is hard to deal with a big issue on a network sitcom. If we are dealing with a big issue, at least we don't have an ad for soap in the middle.

"That longing, aching, confusion, and friendship are why people tune in every week."

WHO NEEDS A HUSBAND? When I started on the show, I was thirty-two and single and felt more of a stigma about being single because all my friends were starting to get married and have kids. But now I feel like these might be the best years of my life, or at least the funniest and most fabulous. When that *Time* magazine cover came out with our four girls on it, with the headline WHO NEEDS A HUSBAND? I remember thinking that the climate had changed for singles, partly because of the show.

ARE WE SLUTS? One season I came back, and I had heard so much feedback from people saying, "These women are sluts, how many men are they going to sleep with?" That notion eventually became an episode, "Are We Sluts?"

With Big and Carrie, we've been acutely aware that people may get fed up if Carrie keeps going back to him, yet people can never get enough of Big. I was talking to someone recently who said, "Big needs to go." A lot of times we address what it feels like people are thinking about the show.

THE WRITERS' BOARD Each year, the writers create a grid of the season on the writers' board, with the four women's names arranged on the left side and the episode numbers and themes written across the top. As the writers fill in plot ideas for particular characters, they work down the board until each

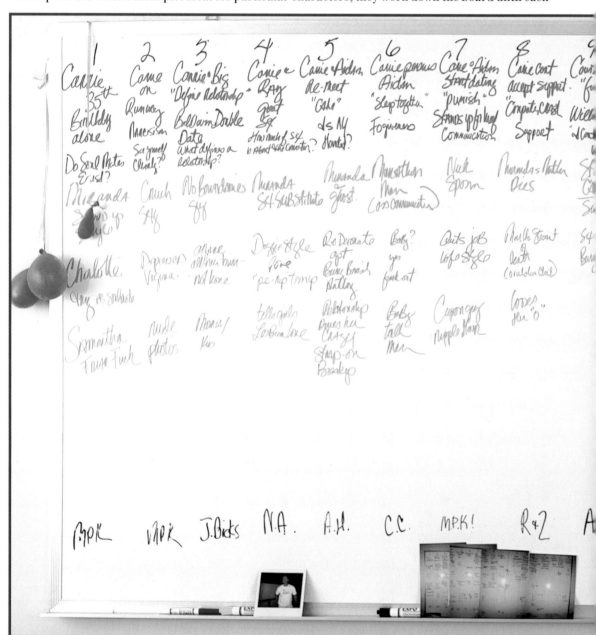

JENNY BICKS
CO-EXECUTIVE PRODUCER

FROM NETWORK TO CABLE When I started writing for *Sex and the City* I had just finished up on *Seinfeld* and I was doing two days a week on *Dawson's Creek*. I saw the pilot and called my agent and said, "I don't know, women don't talk this way." I remember thinking it was too glamorous. By Season Two we brought the women down a bit into reality. I felt that as a woman, I was able to come in and say, "You know what? Maybe a woman would say it a little differently."

"The show talks about fears and loneliness and insecurity and all the things that women in their thirties, twenties, and forties are experiencing."

FEMALE-DRIVEN COMEDY Women tell me they are happy to see that they are not freaks and that this stuff they are experiencing also happens to other women. *Sex and the City* is also a beautiful show to watch. But ultimately, I think the reason it works is because it's real. It's not about the dirty language, it's about the dirty emotion.

WRITERS AND ACTORS Writing this show is great because when the actors are confused or don't understand the intent, they'll just come over and ask you. We are so close on our set that the actors walk up and say, "Hey Jenny, listen, is it okay if I just say it this way?" It's a nice free form that we have. There is always a writer on the set, and it's usually the writer of the episode, because we take everything we write so personally and want to make sure that it's all getting captured. The writers have the tighter connection with the actresses. It's the perfect situation to be in.

episode's stories fit the given theme. They also keep character variety and pacing in mind. "We try to be sure that if one of the characters is in a long-term relationship, at least one character is still single and one is either leaving or starting a relationship," says Amy B. Harris.

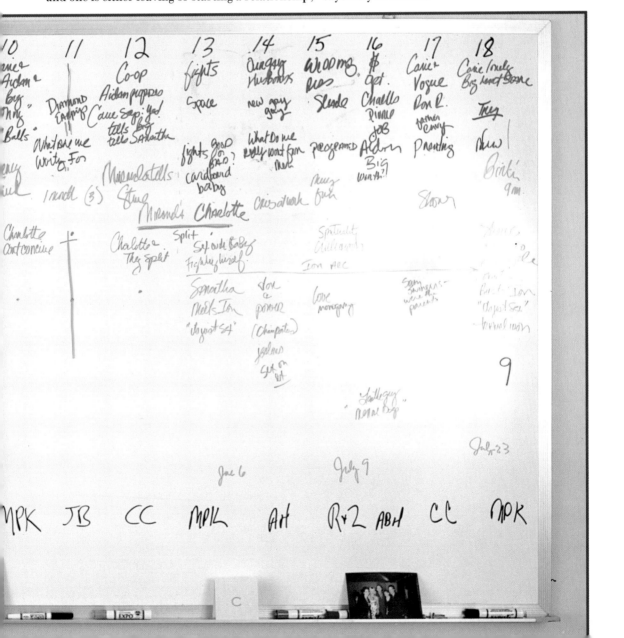

"Who wants to be Mrs. Up the Butt?"
– CHARLOTTE YORK

CHARLOTTE YORK

PLAYED BY KRISTIN DAVIS

When it comes to Charlotte, people tend to have strong opinions. Because she so often espouses a traditional view of men, marriage, and commitment, those who agree with her cheer her on, while those who disagree want to throw things at the television. Charlotte's defining characteristics are her idealism and her perseverance. She always sees the glass as half full and refuses to settle for less than what she deserves. On one level, her needs seem impossible to meet and utterly unrealistic; on another, they are what any woman expects and deserves: love, stability, devotion, and a little trifle called sex.

Over the first two seasons, Charlotte struggled to find a man she could marry who would live up to the fantasy she built for herself as a little girl; yet in her quest to find Prince Charming, she was thwarted again and again. But throughout her travails with Licky-Face Guy, Up-the-Butt Guy, Fall-Asleep Guy, Getting-in-Fights Guy, Yell-During-Sex Guy, and oh so many more, Charlotte stayed resilient, left when she wasn't satisfied, and never lost sight of her dreams. And finally, in the middle of Season Three, she met handsome surgeon Dr. Trey MacDougal, who seemed to be exactly what she wanted.

But as we discovered when they married, Charlotte was in for a few surprises. When she went over to Trey's apartment the night before the wedding, she learned that he couldn't keep the wind in his sails. As she watched her hopes deflate before her very eyes, she refused to check out or give up. Instead, she seemed to grow up. The once *Rules*-y strategist realized that communication was the only solution to their marital problems. Trey offered a hankie; Charlotte offered a list of relationship issues to discuss. He avoided impotency discussions; she attached stamps to his penis at night to see what was causing the problem. She suggested couples therapy, stuck by her desire to have a baby, yelled when she felt he was being insensitive, stood up to his overprotective mother, Bunny, and said they should separate when things weren't going well.

The same character who, in the beginning, seemed so rigid in her opinions of men that we sometimes wanted to shake her by the shoulders, became surprisingly elastic. And when it became clear at the end of Season Four that she and Trey couldn't make it work, she was willing to acknowledge the truth and let him go.

With her openness, honesty, and bravery, Charlotte is in search of that noble but elusive goal: completion. Despite all the challenges she has faced—and will continue to face—somehow it seems like completion is just around the corner.

BIO: Davis's breakthrough role as the devious Brooke Armstrong on the long-running hit series *Melrose Place* first introduced her to television audiences. She has appeared on *Seinfeld*, *The Larry Sanders Show*, and *ER*, and, while shooting *Sex and the City*, guest-starred on *Friends* and *Grosse Point*. She also starred in *25 Days of Christmas* on the Fox Family Channel. Born in Boulder, Colorado, Davis grew up in Columbia, South Carolina, and received her BFA in acting from Rutgers University.

Kristin Davis

MEETING DARREN In 1991 I moved to Los Angeles and worked on a lot of TV shows, and then in 1995 I got cast on *Melrose Place,* which Darren Star was producing. My character, Brooke, was mean but funny at the same time. I really enjoyed it. Then Darren left, and my character changed dramatically. She wasn't funny anymore. She tried to kill herself. I basically had to cry every day at work, and I just hated it. I couldn't even remember my own story lines. We would shoot two shows at once, and sometimes we'd look at each other and say, "Have you cheated on me yet, or was that the one after?"

IT'S ABOUT WHAT? In the beginning my mother was not really thrilled about my being on *Sex and the City.* She was happy I had a job, but she would say things like, "What? It's about what?" She wouldn't watch it for a long time. Her friends liked it and would talk to her about it, so eventually she felt left out. When she began watching, she felt all the guys were jerks and would say, "I don't want to think your life is actually like that." I'd say, "Well, it isn't really, Mom. We're not trying to be every woman. This is a specific Manhattan group of ambitious people."

In the beginning we were worried that some women would feel we were picking on men too much. We were also worried about the right-wing reaction. But I knew it was a show I would want to watch. I felt we needed something with four women who are very different from one another but who are also great friends. What bothered me about *Melrose* was that the female characters were so mean to each other. It was difficult for me to go to work every day and have to call other women "bitch." I hated that. It didn't reflect anyone or any relationship I knew.

I thought *Sex and the City* would be a little cult-type show like *The Larry Sanders Show.* I would have been very happy with that. When we got nominated for the first Emmy, it finally hit me how big the show was. Darren and I used to joke about how we could maybe win a Cable ACE award. That's an award that doesn't even exist anymore.

BIGGER, BIGGER After I got off of *Melrose Place,* I did episodes of *Larry Sanders* and *Seinfeld.* Soon after that I received the script for *Sex and the City.* Charlotte had a very small part in the pilot, but I loved her and asked to audition for that role. I heard they were trying to get Sarah Jessica for Carrie and thought it would be great because I knew she would make it a whole different series.

The day I went in to audition, HBO's computers were down, and I had to wait about five hours before I was called in. They sent me back out after the first read. When I was called back in again, Chris Albrecht, HBO president of original programming, said, "Bigger, bigger," so I did it bigger. I guess it worked.

TURN OF THE TABLES I enjoy watching male guest stars come on our show. What they have to do is something we as women actresses have had to do forever. It's always been part of our lots to come in and do the hot girl. But men aren't used to playing that role. Suddenly the women are in control, and it's about what they think is sexy. It's a complete turn of the tables.

Charlotte doesn't seem like she's in charge, but in many ways she is. She has very high standards. She investigates men. My way of dealing with having her be with so many men is to say to myself, "Okay, yes, Charlotte does go to bed with all these guys, which I probably wouldn't do, but then she is also very quick to say, 'Oh no, he doesn't live up to my standards.'" It might take her a little searching, but Charlotte is hopeful in the face of horrors, and I really like that about her.

KYLE IS KYLE The original story line about Trey was that he would be my incredibly boring husband who the other girls hated, and they wouldn't understand why Charlotte seemed so happy, like in that scene on the boat when Charlotte and Trey are telling Carrie the story of how they met. That was the way their relationship was supposed to be throughout. But Kyle is Kyle. He is not boring, and he is so darn handsome, sexy, interesting, and funny that the writers had to change what they had originally set out for him. That's the wonderful thing about our writers: they roll with what they get.

I didn't get to meet with Kyle when his part was being cast. He just showed up one day. He was described to me as Prince Charming, and I thought, *David Lynch is Prince Charming. Interesting.* I said, "Our relationship is not going to be some sadistic-type thing, is it?"

The Charlotte-Trey story line really got going when we cast Frances Sternhagen. She was not supposed to play as big a part as she eventually did, but she brought so much to the character, and Bunny really helped to make sense of Trey, so the writers just went with it. It was genius on their part.

***MS.* MAGAZINE** The show is really about a cultural movement, which we didn't realize at first. Our generation and those since have grown up with choices. We didn't have to get married by a certain age, we could be career women if we wanted to be. Our mothers didn't have those choices growing up. They were only presented to them later in their lives, when they were already on a certain path. My mother was married when she was twenty and had me when she was twenty-one. I grew up with *Ms.* magazine on the coffee table, but she had already committed to me and my father and to that life. So I think our show is about those choices and about being able to create your life in the way that you want to create it.

When we were on the cover of *Time,* it made me realize that all across the country, not just in New York and L.A., there are more women right now dealing with these issues and with these questions. We have all the things we thought we wanted when we were nineteen. What do we do now? What does it mean to have all these choices?

Our show has gone on longer than we thought it would. We used to say that we would only do four years and that would be it, but none of us wants to quit. I love that we got Miranda pregnant. That brings up a whole new set of problems and circumstances. I love that we can do that with one character and still have Samantha be uninterested in commitment. I love that the four of us are so different, that we can have the variety of choices displayed without saying, "This is the right one" or "This is the wrong one." It's an open book, and we can just continue to explore.

The Rules

BY CHARLOTTE YORK

1
Women really just want to be rescued.

2
No one buys a classic six on the Upper West Side
unless they are seriously thinking about marriage.

3
It's not a rebound when the other person's dead.

4
A vibrator does not call you on your birthday.
A vibrator doesn't send you flowers the day after.
You cannot take a vibrator home to meet your mother.

5
It takes half the total time you went out with someone
to get over them.

6
If you don't have sex for a year, you can actually become
revirginized.

7
I'm very into labels. Gay. Straight.
Pick a side and stay there.

8
When a man has a fantasy and you fulfill it,
there's always the chance the relationship will blow up and
you'll just be the idiot who did it on a golf course.
Or something.

9
WASPs don't yell. It's genetic.

10
The only thing worse than being thirty-four and
single is being thirty-four and divorced.

Season Two was the year *Sex and the City* became a bona fide hit.

Audiences who had only heard about the show through friends during the first season began to tune in on their own. Men who had watched it only reluctantly began sitting down next to their girlfriends and wives each week without shame. And everybody, male or female, began talking about the show at work.

The show's strongest suit continued to be its eye-popping, jaw-dropping comedy. Charlotte tried her hand at a crotch grabber; a gay-straight man; a womanizing widower; and a cocksure movie star. Samantha tried to sustain a relationship with James, but had to admit that size mattered and was forced to say goodbye to her gherkin. In short order, she bedded her trainer; a "déjà fuck" she'd already slept with; and the unforgettable "Flabby Ass."

As Charlotte and Samantha quenched our thirst for water-cooler moments, Miranda and Carrie explored dramatic issues in their long-term relationships. After dating a guy who liked dirty talk except for one vital sentence, Miranda met Steve, a solid, decent guy who forced her to look out the window at the moon. And Carrie, after attempting to get over Big, began seeing him again on the sly. Once she admitted the relationship to the girls, she was forced to admit something more difficult to herself: that nothing had changed about him at all. At the end of the season, she broke up with him before he went off to France, and eventually spotted him in the Hamptons with a knockout twenty-something named Natasha.

In the final, moving episode, "Ex and the City," Carrie had the revelation that Big was like the Robert Redford character, Hubbell, in *The Way We Were*, unable to withstand the complexities of a curly-haired "Katie," and destined to wind up with someone more simple. She went to the Plaza Hotel (where Barbra Streisand and Redford shared their final goodbye), stopped Big on his way out of his engagement party, put her hand on his cheek, and said, "Your girl is lovely, Hubbell." What began as a sad moment became poignantly triumphant: when Big said, "I don't get it," she responded, "And ya never did." As we cried for Carrie and with her, we knew that *Sex and the City* wasn't only about sex but the vulnerability that comes hand in hand with human intimacy.

the gherkin spat, the Twister mat, Miranda's new flat, and the Plaza chat

1

TAKE ME OUT TO THE BALLGAME

WRITTEN BY *michael patrick king*
DIRECTED BY *allen coulter*

"In a world where leaving each other seems to be getting more and more frequent, what are the breakup rules?"
The girls force Carrie out of her post-Big doldrums by dragging her to a Yankees game, where she catches the New Yankee's ball and scores a date; Samantha tries to "coach" James into satisfying her despite his bat size; Charlotte dates a guy who's always adjusting his balls; Miranda tells the girls off for being obsessed with balls and men.

CYNTHIA NIXON (MIRANDA):

After I did that speech about how all we do is talk about men, people came up to me on the street and told me, "I'm so glad you said that!" They felt all the talk about men was the one thing that kept the show from being feminist. But I don't know, that's what our show's about. The women's work is there, but it is fairly peripheral.

2

THE AWFUL TRUTH

WRITTEN BY *darren star*
DIRECTED BY *allen coulter*

"Are there certain things in a relationship that one should never say?"
Carrie encourages a friend to leave her husband—and faces the awful consequences; Samantha and James break up after she admits his penis is too small; Charlotte, convinced a woman's best friend is her dog, purchases a canine; the usually tight-lipped Miranda experiments with pillow talk.

CYNTHIA NIXON:

The dirty-talking scene with the "finger in your ass" guy was one of the more embarrassing scenes. I knew the actor, and he actually called me the day he had been cast because he was nervous about it. He wanted to talk to me about what it would be like, and I think his wife was a little freaked out, too. He asked if he was going to be completely naked, and I said no, not at all.

CARRIE: *Are you really telling us that during sex you're just completely mute?* MIRANDA: *No. I can do a good orgasm alert. You know,*
"I'm gonna come, I'm gonna come, I'm gonna come," but that's because, you know, I'm gonna come.

48

3

FREAKS · GEEKS & STRANGE GIRLS
Sideshow Banners of the Great American Midway

THE FREAK SHOW

WRITTEN BY *jenny bicks*
DIRECTED BY *allen coulter*

"Are all men freaks?"

Carrie dates a series of freaks before meeting a seemingly normal guy, Ben, but ruins it when he finds her searching his place for his "box of freakdom." Charlotte dates a freak named Mr. Pussy; Samantha considers plastic surgery but decides against it; Miranda meets the freaky "Manhattan Guy," who hasn't left the city in ten years.

JENNY BICKS (CO-EXECUTIVE PRODUCER):

I have snooped in a guy's place, although I never got caught doing it. I walked into the writers' room and said, "Ben should catch Carrie snooping, because I've done it." Every guy in the room said, "What are you talking about?" And every woman in the room said, "Duh!" I'm not proud that I have snooped, nor am I saying all women do it, but come on, you leave us alone in your apartment, what do you think is going to happen?

DARREN STAR (CREATOR):

Sometimes the smallest roles are the hardest to cast. Mr. Pussy had only one line but he had to eat a fig and an oyster in the episode. So I had all the actors do their thing on the orange slice. With some of the guys, you wanted to take a shower afterwards, and then we found the one guy who did it in a funny way. The key with all these shows is finding the one guy who will make it funny and not scary.

4

Is Hepatitis C the New AIDS? · Justin Volpe's Lawyer
Death of a Gambler By Steve Fishman

NewYork

Single & Fabulous?
Eat, drink and never-be-married
By Sabrina Wright

THEY SHOOT SINGLE PEOPLE, DON'T THEY?

WRITTEN BY *michael patrick king*
DIRECTED BY *john david coles*

"Is it better to 'fake it' than be alone?"

Carrie does a photo shoot for *New York* magazine, which runs a humiliating picture of her under the headline SINGLE & FABULOUS?; Miranda gets back together with an ex and feels guilty for faking her orgasms; Charlotte tries to fake herself into a romance with a house-handy friend; Samantha dates a phony Latin club owner who professes to be a "we" guy but turns out to be a wee bit of a jerk.

JENNY BICKS:

When we were working on this episode, I had to give an anatomical lesson to Darren. There was an odd moment when I realized he didn't really understand the clitoris, and I had to draw it on the writers' board for him. It was not a proud moment for me. Darren kept saying "in the clitoris" instead of "on." I said, "Why are you saying 'in'? That's not how it works." So I made a big marker drawing with labels on it. It put that one to rest.

CHARLOTTE: *If you really like the guy, what's one little moment of "Ooh! Ooh!" versus spending the whole night in bed alone?*
MIRANDA: *These are my options?*

49

5

FOUR WOMEN AND A FUNERAL

WRITTEN BY *jenny bicks*
DIRECTED BY *allen coulter*

"In a world where everyone's dying to make a connection, can a relationship bring you back to life?"

After the women attend a fashion designer's funeral, Big and Carrie go bowling and resuscitate their relationship; Charlotte dates a widower who two-times her with other sympathetic women; Samantha gets exiled from the Manhattan social scene after she hits on a married philanthropist; Miranda has panic attacks after buying her own apartment.

JENNY BICKS:

I bought a house in L.A. and I had to keep checking these boxes for "single woman." It dawned on me that you can get to the point where you have enough money, enough security, and enough independence to buy your own house, but they still make you continually tell them you are single.

CYNTHIA NIXON:

That hospital scene is maybe my favorite we've ever done. It was the first time Miranda admitted that she is shaky about her world. Allen Coulter, who is one of our wonderful directors, directed it after we had shot the Mr. Pussy scene from "The Freak Show" in the bathroom, which he filmed in some very inventive way. When we came to the hospital scene, I was nervous because I viewed it as quite emotional from the beginning, and he was worried he had neglected it and hadn't thought of a clever way to film it, but I loved it.

6

THE CHEATING CURVE

WRITTEN BY *darren star*
DIRECTED BY *john david coles*

"Is cheating like the proverbial tree in the forest— it doesn't exist if there's no one around to catch you?"

Carrie finds herself cheating on her friends with Mr. Big; Charlotte meets a group of Power Lesbians and tries to convince herself she is emotionally gay; Miranda dates a guy who watches porn while they're in bed; Samantha gets a "lightning bolt" from her personal trainer.

CHARLOTTE: *While sexually I feel that I am straight, there's a very powerful part of me that connects to the female spirit.*
PATTY (POWER LESBIAN): *Sweetheart, that's all very nice, but if you're not going to eat pussy, you're not a dyke.*

Wedding Poem
by Carrie Bradshaw

His hello was the end of her endings.
Her laugh was their first step down the aisle.
His hand would be hers to hold forever.
His forever was as simple as her smile.

An ocean couldn't prevent it.
A New York minute wouldn't let it pass.
Does the Universe decide for us
Which love will fade and which love will last?

He said she was what was missing.
She said instantly she knew.
She was a question to be answered
And his answer was, "I do".

7

THE CHICKEN DANCE

WRITTEN BY *cindy chupack*
DIRECTED BY *victoria hochberg*

"In a city as cynical as New York, is it still possible to believe in love at first sight?"

A male friend of Miranda's falls in love with her decorator, and when they get married, Miranda has to be the guest-book girl. Charlotte meets a guy at the wedding and goes through an entire relationship over the course of the evening. Carrie, asked by the couple to read a poem, cries in the middle of it over Big's commitment-phobia and has to pretend her tears are happy ones. And Samantha has a déjà fuck.

CINDY CHUPACK (CO-EXECUTIVE PRODUCER)**:**

There was a lot of debate up until the last minute about the bouquet. I originally thought Carrie should–for the first time in her life–try to catch it, but Darren and Michael really believed that the bouquet should just fall to the floor in front of these women. That episode was reviewed, and someone wrote how nice it was that the ending was not the cliché leap for the bouquet. Darren and Michael were right, and it was a very *Sex and the City* moment. It took some relearning for me to realize that these women were hopeful and yet still sort of cynical and dry. The show has evolved in the same way that bouquet moment did–marriage isn't necessarily the be-all and end-all.

8

THE MAN, THE MYTH, THE VIAGRA

WRITTEN BY *michael patrick king*
DIRECTED BY *victoria hochberg*

"Are we willing to believe anything to date?"

Carrie asks Big to get to know her friends; Miranda, on the verge of giving up on men entirely, meets a sweet bartender named Steve; and Donald Trump appears on the show, as does a bare, geriatric male ass (though not Donald Trump's).

DARREN STAR:

The flabby ass was not the actual ass of the actor who played the older man. He was the ass double. I asked his wife why he wanted to do it and his wife said, "He's always wanted to break into show business." He was a seventy-five-year-old retired guy, and it was his first big break.

JOE COLLINS (FIRST ASSISTANT CAMERA)**:**

We shot the scene with the old guy's butt in the presidential suite of the Plaza Hotel. The Plaza had given the room key to the show for the weekend, and this guy in the camera department and his wife decided to take advantage of the room one evening. They were in there in full swing when they heard a knock at the door. Victoria, the director, had come to scout the room over the weekend and busted them in the middle of the tryst. But they were able to scramble and work themselves into some clothing, and make it seem that they were there for production purposes!

MIRANDA: *I can't have dinner with you. I don't even know you.* **STEVE:** *You slept with me!* **MIRANDA:** *It's a different thing!*

CHARLOTTE: *He's getting circumcised.* CARRIE: *Please tell me that we're not invited to the bris.*

9

OLD DOGS, NEW DICKS

WRITTEN BY *jenny bicks*
DIRECTED BY *alan taylor*

"Can you change a man?"
Carrie tries to get Big to stop looking at other women when he's around her; Charlotte dates an uncut man who's willing to circumscribe his goals to hers; Miranda wants Steve to accommodate her schedule; Samantha bumps into an old boyfriend who's now a drag queen.

JENNY BICKS:

I had a boyfriend who called me up and said, "Do me a favor. Go look at the moon." That is the kind of person who makes you stop and look at the world and stop running so far away from them. The episode was about whether you can change a man, but ultimately it was about how you can't really change a man or a woman but you can let someone see a different side of life. That's what Steve did for Miranda, and ultimately what this guy did for me.

10

THE CASTE SYSTEM

WRITTEN BY *darren star*
DIRECTED BY *allison anders*

"Can we date outside our caste?"
Steve and Miranda break up because of class differences; Samantha dates a man of such high caste he has a servant; Charlotte gets cast as a movie star's groupie; Big takes Carrie to a Park Avenue soirée—and Carrie realizes he has no idea who she really is.

KRISTIN DAVIS (CHARLOTTE):

Brian Van Holt, who played the movie star, had to say that bad line about what Charlotte should do in the bathroom ["stick your finger in your pussy"]. For a long time, until I got Kyle, every man Charlotte went out with was a really, really horrible person. Brian is the sweetest thing in the world and very committed to his girlfriend. Every time he had to say that, he could barely get it out before he'd start apologizing. They would have just called cut, and he'd say to me, "I'm sorry! I'm sorry!"

MR. BIG: *Listen. I know what you're really pissed off about. But it's just something I've gotta do in my own time! Okay? Well, I fucking love you! All right? You know I do. . . . But it's just a tough thing for me to say, because it always seems to get me in trouble . . . when I say it. Okay?* CARRIE: *Okay.*

11

EVOLUTION

WRITTEN BY *cindy chupack*
DIRECTED BY *pam thomas*

"Are New Yorkers evolving past relationships?"

Carrie tries, unsuccessfully, to leave a few feminine items at Big's; Miranda's gynecologist tells her she has a lazy ovary; Charlotte can't decide what side of the banquet table her pastry-chef beau sits on; Samantha tries to take revenge on an ex but gets beaten to the punch.

KRISTIN DAVIS:

My first sex scene on the show was with Dan Futterman, the actor in this episode. It was important to the story line that you could see Charlotte have all these orgasms. It was interesting that this guy who seemed gay would be this great lover. That's the thing about sex, you can never quite tell.

CINDY CHUPACK:

There were a lot of references to evolution in the script, but Pam Thomas, the director, figured out exactly what I was trying to do with the words and then magnified it. There's a scene where Mr. Big opens the medicine chest and finds a bunch of Carrie's things in there and it was Pam's idea that she start from the back of the mirror and make it look like he was a caveman. The editor, Michael Berenbaum, and music supervisor, Dan Lieberstein, added a lot of music that reflected that, like drums and tribal sounds.

12

LA DOULEUR EXQUISE!

WRITTEN BY *ollie levy &
michael patrick king*
DIRECTED BY *allison anders*

"When it comes to relationships, how do you know when enough is enough?"

Big tells Carrie he's moving to Paris for six months; Samantha takes the girls to a new S & M restaurant; Charlotte meets a shoe-store foot fetishist willing to make a trade; Miranda meets a guy who likes to "do it" only when he might get caught.

BEHIND-THE-SCENES TIDBIT:

In this episode, Stanford goes to an after-hours gay club in the meatpacking district where guests are required to take off their pants before entering. The idea for this came from writer-director Michael Patrick King, who had gone to a party where guests were asked to check their clothes at the door.

WILLIE GARSON (STANFORD)**:**

The underwear-bar scene was the first time they had gotten me out of my clothing. I was so nervous. I thought the extras would be all these big, muscled, hunky guys, which is how they would show a gay bar on any other TV show. This bar was full of normal-looking guys in their underwear, which was very comforting.

13

GAMES PEOPLE PLAY

WRITTEN BY *jenny bicks*
DIRECTED BY *michael spiller*

"Do you have to play games to make a relationship work?"
Carrie decides to try therapy and, in the waiting room, winds up meeting Seth (Jon Bon Jovi); Samantha dates a sports addict who woos only when his team wins; Miranda plays "peep show" with a man in the building across from her.

JEREMY CONWAY (PRODUCTION DESIGNER):

One of the biggest fights I ever had was about what the floor in Carrie's apartment would be. If the shooting crew had their way, it would be a concrete floor because you can dolly on it and not hit a bump. I wanted to put down a hardwood oak floor. Everybody said, "You can't do that. It will slow down the shoots, and we'll never see it." But this episode was my opportunity because Jon Bon Jovi and Sarah Jessica had to play Twister on the floor. We're one of the few TV shows where a lot of people do end up on the floor.

14

THE FUCK BUDDY

WRITTEN BY *darren star & merrill markoe*
DIRECTED BY *alan taylor*

"Are we all, in fact, just dating the same person over and over again?"
Carrie makes a date with her fuck buddy; Samantha "makes love" with the couple on the other side of her wall; Charlotte starts double-booking her dates and faces the logistical consequences; Miranda dates a mean guy whose obnoxiousness is unsexy in life but not in bed.

BEHIND-THE-SCENES TIDBIT:

Carrie's fuck buddy was played by Dean Winters, Ryan O'Reily on HBO's prison drama, *Oz.*

SAMANTHA: *You can't date your fuck buddy. . . . You're going to take the only person in your life that's there purely for sex, no strings attached, and turn him into a human being? Why?*

54

CHARLOTTE (TO SAMANTHA): *Is your vagina in the New York City guidebooks? Because it should be! It's the hottest spot in town! It's always open!*

FRESH
SHIRTS
On
Tuesday

~A~
Collection
of SHORT
STORIES
by
VAUGHN
WEISEL

15

SHORTCOMINGS

WRITTEN BY *terri minsky*
DIRECTED BY *dan algrant*

"When you sleep with someone, are you screwing the family?"

Carrie dates a short-story writer who has problems working in longer formats—but then she falls in love with his family (who wouldn't, when the mom is TV's Rhoda, Valerie Harper?). Miranda dates a divorced father but has trouble getting along with his kid; Charlotte's brother comes to town, and Samantha makes him feel at home.

MICHAEL PATRICK KING (EXECUTIVE PRODUCER):

The biggest mistake ever was bringing Charlotte's brother on. It was good for the story because Charlotte got to say that line about Samantha's vagina being in the New York City guidebooks, and they got to have the beginning of their crisis. But I realized when I saw a family member on the show that I probably never want to see another one because it can never live up to the audience's imagination of who these people are. How much do you really know your friends' families if you live in New York City?

BEHIND-THE-SCENES TIDBIT:

Justin Theroux, who played the role of Vaughn, the short-story writer in "Shortcomings," also appeared in "The Monogamists" in Season One, as Jared, a novelist Carrie flirts with when she finds out Big is dating other women.

16

WAS IT GOOD FOR YOU?

WRITTEN BY *michael patrick king*
DIRECTED BY *dan algrant*

"How do you know if you're good in bed?"

Carrie dates a recovering alcoholic who says she's the best sex he's ever had; Charlotte drags the girls to a tantric-sex workshop; Samantha tries a threesome with two gay friends; Miranda tries to change her bed karma.

MICHAEL PATRICK KING:

Anytime anyone gets highfalutin about anything on the show, they get cream-pied by the guys, like in the tantric-sex scene. The way that plotline evolved was that I had bumped into a guy in a health-food market who told me he had just been in a tantric-sex workshop and that it was an older couple who led it. He said that when the guy came, "There were ropes and ropes of come." That image stuck in my mind, and I thought, *Well then, it could probably fly across the room and hit Miranda.*

JOE COLLINS:

The woman who was playing the tantric-sex woman is a respected Polish actress, and her English isn't a hundred percent. She thought she was actually going to have to masturbate this guy on screen. It wasn't until she got on set that we explained to her that we could fake it with the camera angle. She collapsed in relief.

17

Nina G. Public Relations
Invites you to attend the Annual
Hampton Hoedown
Wear your best Sunday-Go-To-Meetin' Duds

Sasparilla
Vittles
Line and Square Dancin'
Fireworks

20-SOMETHING GIRLS VS. 30-SOMETHING WOMEN

WRITTEN AND DIRECTED BY *darren star*

"Twenty-something girls: friend . . . or foe?"

The girls get a Hamptons share; Samantha's assistant quits, steals her Rolodex, and throws the party of the summer; Charlotte dates a twenty-something guy who gives her crabs; Carrie sees Big with Natasha, a twenty-six-year-old he's met in Paris.

SARAH JESSICA PARKER (CARRIE):

This episode is a really nice example of Darren's writing. We all go to the Hamptons, and we are in this house, and it's silly and ridiculous and awful, and it's not what we want it to be. Then Carrie's on the beach in a cowboy hat, and she's feeling all up in her stuff, and then she turns around and there's Big. Then she regains her composure and slips back into her routine with him, where it's pithy. And he's with Natasha and it's as if he says, "Here she is and this is my life, and we met, and I kind of lied to you about what I wanted and didn't want." And Carrie's in a cowboy hat and a bra and an old Kenzo skirt and she throws up. She feels actually physically ill from it. That's classic Darren Star writing. It leads you for twenty-six minutes on a romp in the Hamptons for a weekend, and then in that last moment, it all changes.

18

EX AND THE CITY

WRITTEN AND DIRECTED BY *michael patrick king*

"Can you be friends with an ex?"

Big tells Carrie he and Natasha are engaged; Miranda and Steve go out as friends and wind up as more; Samantha meets Mr. Cocky, who turns out to be a little too big for his britches; Charlotte, upset over a childhood horse-riding accident, tries to get back in the saddle.

MICHAEL PATRICK KING:

When Carrie was going to meet Big for lunch in this episode, I had written that she had a shoulder bag that gets caught on the chair as she walks away and pulls the chair over. I knew it had to be a shoulder bag because, in order for the comedy to work, she had to get two steps away and yank. So I tell Sarah Jessica about the shoulder bag, and she says, "No one is doing shoulder bags." But then she called me up the next day and said, "Fendi is showing a shoulder bag." I thought, *Whew! We can do the show because Fendi is showing a shoulder bag!*

SABRINA WRIGHT (PROPERTY MASTER):

In this episode Carrie gets an invitation to Big and Natasha's engagement party, and on the announcement, because Big doesn't have a name, I wrote, "Boris and Natasha wish to announce their wedding." Sarah Jessica read it and nearly fell on the floor laughing.

MIRANDA: *How could you not have seen* The Way We Were? **SAMANTHA:** *Chick film.*

Sets and the City

The sets of *Sex and the City* are constructed to feel as true-to-life as the writing and all other aspects of production. Jeremy Conway, the show's production design, is responsible for designing any sets that are used, including the coffee shop and each of the women's apartments. Conway works closely with his set decorator, Karin Wiesel, to make sure the apartments feel right for their characters and authentically New York. "The sets enable you to get color theory going," Conway explains. "Samantha's color scheme is like a big-game hunter, ochres and reds. Charlotte is kind of ivory tower, whites and very atonal. Miranda is like the color of a bruise, with plums and greens. Carrie is a soft sea-foam teal color, which works great for her skin tone and her hair." Follow Conway on a behind-the-scenes tour of the realistic, striking, and detailed sets of *Sex and the City* . . .

JEREMY CONWAY: Carrie's apartment is an apartment everybody's had. The idea was that instead of the bed being in a separate bedroom, the apartment is one big room with curtains that you can pull. The closet is more like a hallway to the bathroom, with racks in it for all her clothes, because the most important thing to Carrie is what she wears. If shooting is taking place in the closet, then we really try to show clothes that you've seen Carrie in before to make it more real. We change the magazines on a regular basis, we rotate books and the stuff inside the drawers. If Carrie is reading a book in bed in a scene, we carefully decide what book it is she's reading. All the floors are hardwood and the forty-year-old braided telephone wire painted into the wall is very typical of Manhattan rental apartments. The photos on her refrigerator and bookshelf are all personal photos of Sarah Jessica's friends and her friend's daughter.

Carrie

Samantha

Samantha's apartment was easy to design because her character was so broadly defined in the first season. When we moved her to the meatpacking district, she got a bed on wheels. We went for a converted-warehouse look. We built the mantel and tried to make it modern and perfectly proportioned. It has candles on top in a red boat of glass holders. We wanted the kitchen to be part of the selling point of the apartment. The counter that separates the living space from the kitchen has the sink built into it, and there is lots of shelving up above. Of course, the kitchen is totally wasted on Samantha, except for the time she and Maria made spaghetti together. There is a door for the bathroom, but only a big, large gauze that hangs behind her bed that separates where you come in from the main living area. The bathroom has green-slate tile, a built-in tub, and cantilevered sink that looks like a little bowl.

We use a lot of hard edges and lines for Miranda. She is a very complex character, and a lot is below the surface, so we thought that would be a good thing to exploit in terms of design. When Miranda bought her new place, she had a designer do her kitchen, even though she doesn't know how to cook. But she knew that it was important to have all the right gear. We carried the idea of the bruise palette into the kitchen, with the backsplash-tile combination and the countertops. There is a faceted mirror over the mantel, a starburst. That is really right for her character because it is multifaceted and reflects a lot of different things, like Miranda's different sides. Items that are more revealing of Miranda's character are back in the bedroom. She has sheer curtains and surprisingly feminine touches, like antique perfume bottles, candles, and some family photographs on the dresser, including a childhood photo of Cynthia.

Miranda

Charlotte

Before Charlotte moved in with Trey, her bedroom was all white. The molding and trims were similar to Upper West Side prewar buildings, and it had parquet floors. When Charlotte moved in with Trey, we knew there was going to be a struggle against Bunny, and that Charlotte's independence was going to manifest itself in the apartment's being redecorated. It really shocked Bunny when she came in and saw Charlotte taking down the drapes. We gave the apartment a more modern look and everything became more vertical and less horizontal. All the walls in the passageway went white and we had more trim added to them as well. As for the baby room, who in their right mind would really start doing a baby room if you are not even pregnant? It had all the right murals on the wall, but it was so awful in that moment where Charlotte comes in and looks at it. It was completed just in time for Charlotte to walk out of the marriage.

CARRIE

SAMANTHA

MIRANDA

CHARLOTTE

If one aspect of the show epitomizes its courageousness and outrageousness, it is the fashion. What began as a whimsical and necessary asset to an already strong series has evolved into a style bible so trendsetting that its influence can be seen all over the country. Items that appear in episodes (a flower on the lapel, Ray-Ban aviator sunglasses, and a nameplate necklace) zoom into popular culture faster than a midtown taxi.

Though audiences are obsessed with the outfits of all the female characters, Carrie's style is most emblematic of the envelope-pushing wardrobe. With her eclectic mix of name-brand designers and vintage chic, Sarah Jessica Parker has swiftly become television's most influential fashionista. The clothes can be so fantastical it can be hard to believe that anyone would wear them in real life, but as costume designer Patricia Field, who has fire-engine-red hair, will tell you, "I'm here to entertain. The show is not a documentary. Its success is that it elevates itself a bit above reality."

"I wanted fashion to be really important in this show," creator Darren Star recalls. "I wrote an episode of *90210* in its first season, showed it to some friends, and was amazed to find that women watched the shows for clothes as much as the story."

Parker, always fashion-conscious and beautifully stylish, was similarly insistent that the wardrobe be true to New York and up-to-date. "I knew that the fashion wasn't there yet in the pilot," she says. "I knew the clothes were important because I knew women in the city looked a certain way. They don't look like women in other cities, and that doesn't mean they all look like each other, either."

Star, Parker, and first-season producer Barry Jossen agreed that Field would be the designer to lend the show the New York street cred it needed. Though Field had worked as a costume designer in film and television for over fifteen years, she was unique in also being an urban clothier. Her eponymous boutique, which has been at its current Greenwich Village location since 1971, is known for freewheeling, playful clothes that cater to club hoppers, kids, and habitués of downtown New York.

"Pat Field has been here her whole life," says Parker, "and she's been an icon in the fashion industry for almost as long as she's been working in it. I knew the fashion on the show had to be special. It didn't mean that people would like it, but it had to be special."

Back in 1998, when the show started, no one involved had an idea of the hullabaloo to come. Star feels the fashion's impact makes an ironic commentary on conformity itself: "Carrie is a character whose style is dictated by whimsy. She dresses distinctively and would not be wearing a flower if everybody else was. The funniest thing about fashion is that if real people are wearing something, the fashionistas won't because they can't be doing what the rest of the public is doing."

"None of us knew that fashion would have an impact in any way beyond being an important part of the show," says Parker. "That's why we have to be careful that we don't do things just to do them. It's like taking candy from a baby. You have to be careful not to take advantage of that."

Of her often eclectic costume decisions, Field acknowledges that certain items can be controversial. "Sometimes we have to explain our choices because it hasn't been seen before. But that's how you get it to look special. If you just put the expected there, then it's not going to have that panache."

Carrie
Carries Apt.

Carrie
INT. Cafe

Carrie
INT. Miranda's Apt./Livingroom

A CONVERSATION WITH

Patricia Field

THE TRIANGLE The formula I use is an equidistant triangle. One point of the triangle is the actor, another is the character, and the third is the wardrobe. Each of these points caters to the script. When you design a look for a show, your responsibility is to make the actor feel the most comfortable and believable to himself or herself as the character. If the actor is distracted by her clothing, then you are doing her a huge disservice. To best do this, we have a strong creator who has a vision, we have an initial communication about who the characters are and what they represent, and then we meet with the actors and familiarize ourselves with them.

I find costumes in a variety of places. I would say that about forty percent of the wardrobe is borrowed and the rest is bought. In the opener of Season Four, "The Agony and the 'Ex'-Tacy," Sarah Jessica was wearing a little blue cape. I picked that up in a thrift shop in Miami. It was about five dollars. The costumes on the show range from that to twenty-thousand dollars.

I also go to the couture shows in Paris, which is fun because everything from them is made to order. That's how we found the Givenchy dress Carrie wears when she goes to the Monkey Bar with Big. I had been to the couture show in January and brought back all the photos. We found it while going through them with Sarah Jessica, and they sent us the dress from Paris. Any expensive pieces like that, we have to send back to the designer when we're done.

My favorite shots involve the four girls, because to me that's a time when I can editorialize, when the four are walking down the street or making an entrance together. Like when they were walking out of the hotel in L.A., or at the Yankees game, or when they were on the Staten Island Ferry going to the fireman calendar competition.

THE LIFE OF A COSTUME PIECE There is always a gap between when we shoot and when a show airs, and the gap closes as the season progresses. But we don't worry about costumes being out of date by the time a show airs. We just play it for the moment. When we finish an episode, the actresses can choose to purchase anything that has been bought. A lot of times the pieces get auctioned, either at a benefit or on the HBO website. A white shirt of Mr. Big's went for a lot of money, as did the sequined American-flag bag Carrie had in "The Agony and the 'Ex'-Tacy."

THE FASHION MAGAZINE In the beginning, designers were cooperative, but we now have huge access, especially when it comes to the couture. The designers are great to us. Sarah Jessica is like a supermodel, and for her to wear the clothing on the show is important to the designers. Sarah Jessica is very involved in what she wears. She brings things in as ideas. She looks at every magazine. We show her all of the "look" books from the different designers, the books that show all the

Carrie
SS AOT

Carrie
Plaza Hallway

Carrie
Plaza Hallway

runway outfits. She is a very fashionable person, and her interest helps us do our job.

Kristin often brings in pictures of things she likes or actual pieces that she gets from different designers that she wants to wear. Cynthia likes to wear personal jewelry. In one of the episodes, Kim wore a lavender sweater set that belonged to her. These women have been playing these characters for four seasons, and so, in terms of fashion, they and their characters blend more and more over time.

REALITY VERSUS FICTION

I never worry that Carrie's wardrobe doesn't make sense for a writer's income, because I rationalize that she lives in Manhattan, knows designers, and can walk into a showroom and borrow what she wants. Also, she is a bright girl. She can go to thrift shops and mix things up, which she does. She is interested in looking the way she looks, and she puts her energy into figuring out a way to do it. Miranda, who has more money than Carrie, doesn't dress as fashionably. It's not always about the money. It's really about the desire. But ultimately, I don't think about it. I can walk off the reality tightrope a little, as long as I don't fall down.

LINGERIE AND FEET

We have a lot of fun with the lingerie. Samantha wears black and colored lingerie, always a rich color, a red or purple. Charlotte wears black and white or black and pink. Carrie usually wears black, but she also wears quirky things like the Calvin Klein boys' underwear.

Carrie also wears black bras under white T-shirts. It shows the bra. A bra is underwear, but a T-shirt used to be, too. Before 1950 no man or woman would have worn a T-shirt out in public because that was underwear. Once James Dean and Marlon Brando did it, the T-shirt became the most common form of a top for everyone. I see the bra the same way. It is not something that needs to be hidden.

The foot is a very good place to work the sexy look, and we've got all the girls in high heels now. In the beginning, Sarah Jessica wanted to wear them because she loves them, and the success of her in heels really convinced everybody that none of the characters should wear clunky shoes or flats.

THE IMPACT Everybody wants to watch the show and see what the girls are wearing. People get together, have dinner, and watch the show. Working on this show has made me understand more and more the power of television to communicate, which is one of the reasons that I enjoy working in television. If you have something to say, you have the opportunity to say it to millions to people. That's exciting to me.

Carrie

"I feel that Sarah Jessica takes her little fashion trips through the character of Carrie," says Patricia Field. "Carrie dresses more quirkily than Sarah Jessica, but that quirkiness is in Sarah Jessica, and she expresses it through Carrie."

"Pat gives me credit for things that may have been her ideas, and I give her credit for things that I think in the end were maybe my ideas," says Parker. "We just work really well together. I have a tremendous amount of respect for her. It's just a great environment, and when environments are conducive to creativity, good things and silly things come from that."

Parker feels it's right for the characters that the wardrobe seem self-conscious. "I think it's fraudulent for us to pretend, 'Really? You like what I'm wearing? I hadn't given it a thought.' I don't think that's true, and I especially don't think it's true with Carrie. Carrie loves clothes, shoes, and purses, and she has probably been obsessed with fashion from the time she was a very little girl and went to the library with her class and looked at *Seventeen* magazine. The clothes are fun, exciting, and intentionally provocative, and they tell a story."

Sometimes not everyone on the set agrees about a given fashion choice. One of the more controversial items over the history of the show was the "Heidi" dress that Carrie wore to lunch in the park with her friends for Season Two's "The Fuck Buddy." "It's been spoken of as too extreme and self-conscious," Parker recalls. "It became the example for when we've gone too far. I take total blame for that, but I also stand by that. It's a great example of Carrie dressing for an occasion. She's going to a picnic in the park with her friends, so she's got a big heavy brocade blanket, and she found a dirndl. I even had Kabuki, the makeup artist, put freckles on my face. You have to take chances like that if you're going to have a character who is in love with silhouettes and colors and textures and fashion."

DRESS: *Tracy Feith*
FLOWER: *Chanel*
BAG: *Fendi*

DRESS: *vintage*
BAG: *Fendi*
SHOES: *vintage*

SWEATER: *Agnès B.*
SKIRT: *Prada*
COAT: *Marni*

PLAYSUIT: *Pierrot*
COAT: *Prada*
SHOES: *Fendi*

DRESS: *Celine*
COAT: *Momo Falana*
SHOES:
Christian Louboutin

COAT: *silk tre*
SHOES: *Isaac M*

Sometimes disagreements center on whether a given wardrobe choice tells too much about a scene. "Michael Patrick King and I sometimes disagree about when it's appropriate to say stuff with fashion and when it's not. He has very strong opinions, and generally he wins. Whether you win or lose is not the point. You get closer every time to some kind of new truth."

Parker also feels that a sense of fantasy is true to Carrie's character. "In the top of the fourth season, I wore that Givenchy dress to the Monkey Bar with Big," she recalls. "I loved walking in like that with him. I just thought it immediately illustrated the moment so well. People saw that dress and said, 'She's going to wear that huge dress?' I said, 'Yeah, she's going to wear that huge dress, and we're going to walk in the door, he's going to hold the door for me, touch the small of my back, usher me into the room, and light my cigarette. It's going to be great and glamorous circa 1940.'"

Parker's own sensibility has influenced her character's in many ways, such as Carrie's tendency to wear bras in bed. "When I met with Darren Star," she recalls, "I said, 'You will never see me with my clothes off.' He said, 'Fine, end of story.' I don't feel comfortable doing nudity, but I didn't want to have sheets up to my neck all the time so I thought, *I'll just wear bras to bed.*"

Parker had heard that Marilyn Monroe wore bras to bed and felt the choice could help support Carrie's old-fashioned style. "She really believes, in a literary way, in the idea of love, so I thought there was something pure and chaste about wearing bras to bed."

As for how her outer wardrobe has influenced her life, Parker opts to purchase many of Carrie's clothes, which she either wears, keeps in her closet, or auctions off. Whatever she may do with the clothing, Parker clearly relishes the opportunity to be fashionably whimsical as Carrie. "You have to take chances with the fashion, just like you do in the writing. And if we make mistakes, then we make mistakes. It's just a television show."

DRESS:
Badgley Mischka
EARRINGS: *antique*

CAPE: *vintage*
SHIRT: *Moschino*
BUSTIER: *Chloe*
SKIRT: *Prada*

TOP: *Chanel*
EARRINGS:
"Carrie" hoops

GREEN NECLACE:
Christina Caruso
SHIRT: *6969*

TOP: *Liz Collins*
SKIRT: *Vivienne Westwood*

TOP: *Chanel*
JACKET: *Chanel*
SKIRT: *Chanel*

TOP AND SKIRT: *Prada*
BAG: *Gucci*
SHOES: *Manolo Blahnik*

TUNIC: *vintage*
JACKET: *Marni*
NECKLACE: *Bulgari*

DRESS: *vintage*
SHOES: *Manolo Blahnik*
BAG: *Coach*

DRESS: *Roberto Cavalli*
SHOES: *Halston*

TOP: *tube top over
Calvin Klein bra*
SHORTS: *Bebe*
FLIP-FLOPS: *J. Crew*

TOP: *House of Fi*
BAG: *Fendi*

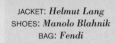

DRESS: *vintage*
SHOES: *Manolo Blahnik*
WATCH: *Piajet*

DRESS: *Mari Mekko*
BAG: *Valentino*
SHOES: *Manolo Blahnik*

TOP: *Chloe*
SKIRT: *Vivienne Westwood*
SHOES:
Manolo Blahnik

JUMPSUIT: *Chaiken*
BOOTS: *Casadei*

JACKET: *Helmut Lang*
SHOES: *Manolo Blahnik*
BAG: *Fendi*

JACKET: *beige su*
SWEATER: *Cather*

TOP: *lexander McQueen*
AWL: handknit

TOP: *cowl neck pullover*
BELT: *leopard chain*

JACKET: *Bergdorf Goodman*

JACKET: *Marni*
PANTS: *Chloe*
BAG: *Christian Dior*

DRESS: *vintage*

DRESS: *Ete*

RESS: *Prada*
: *Manolo Blahnik*
HOE IN HAND:
ar de la Renta

DRESS: *vintage*
EARRINGS: *Chanel*

TOP AND SKIRT: *Prada*
COAT: *Jean Charles de Castelbajac*
BAG: *Fendi*

TOP: *Dolce & Gabbana*
JEANS: *DK*
SHOES: *Candies*

NIGHTGOWN: *vintage*

DRESS: *Azzedine Alaia*
BAG: *Miu Miu*
SHOES: *Manolo Blahnik*

SHOES:
stian Louboutin

CARDIGAN: *Marni*
JEANS: *Earl*
SHOES:
Manolo Blahnik

DRESS: *Richard Tyler*
SHOES: *vintage*

DRESS: *vintage*
JEWELRY: *Mia & Lizzy*
SHOES:
Manolo Blahnik

SUIT: *Vivienne Westwood*
SHOES: *Manolo Blahnik*

DRESS: *Celine*
BAG: *Bulgari*
SHOES: *Christian Louboutin*

Samantha

"Samantha is a lot of fun to dress," says Patricia Field, "because she is such a vivid and sexual character, and she is very open about her attitude toward her sex life. And, because she owns her own company, she can dress how she chooses." Her attire, as Field describes it, consists of "bright-colored suits, fitted waistlines, low-cut necklines, loud jewelry. It's over the top and in your face, on the Versace edge. It's like Versace goes to work or Versace goes to bed, and it's more theatrical than any of the other characters' wardrobes."

"What I have learned from Pat Field," says Kim Cattrall, "is to have a sense of humor about costuming, and not have it be a hindrance, but a fun asset to what you're doing."

Cattrall says that early on in the series, she felt that Samantha needed to wear more of-the-moment clothing, but Field taught her that outfits could be eclectic. "She would put outfits together not from one or two designers but from six designers, and one from '78 and one from '86. At the beginning of every season, she would say, 'Let's do a Joan Collins thing,' or

TOP: *Daryl K.*
JEANS: *Guess*
SHOES: *Manolo Blahnik*

DRESS:
Diane von Furstenberg
JEWELRY: *Harry Winston*
BROOCH: *Swarovski*

SHIRT: *Iceberg*
BAG: *Valentino*
SHOES: *Sergio Rossi*

BAG: *Fendi*

DRESS: *Thierry Mugler*
BAG: *Valentino*
JEWELRY:
Harry Winston

HAT: *Lulu Guin*
TOP: *548*
PANTS: *Trina T*
SHOES: *Jimmy C*

'Let's do a Kim Novak thing.' There were these homages."

In life, Cattrall says, about a quarter to a third of her own wardrobe comes from the show. However, like the other actresses, she does not always wear the clothes she buys. "I come from a very rural background," she says, "and when I'm not in the city, I'm in jeans or khakis or very comfortable clothing. So a lot of the wardrobe does not work for my lifestyle. Sometimes I'll take a few suits or one or two dresses, but then when I wear them, people say, 'Oh yeah, you wore that on such-and-such episode.'"

Cattrall says that Field's and Sarah Jessica Parker's excitement for fashion has been infectious. "Now I look at fashion magazines, and instead of thinking, *Oh my God, I could never wear that*, I think, *This is a fantasy*. The fashion represents not just a character but also the time we're living in. It's been an education for me."

S: *Roberto Cavalli*
SHOES:
iuseppe Zanotti

JEANS: *Roberto Cavalli*
BAG: *Louis Vuitton*
SHOES: *Versace*

COAT: *short fur*
GLOVES:
cream leather

DRESS: *Yigal Azrouel*
SHOES:
Giuseppe Zanotti

PANTSUIT:
Emanuel Ungaro
BAG: *Chanel*

SHOES:
Manolo Blahnik

Charlotte

Charlotte's style is the most classic and reserved of the women—solids mixed with pretty patterns; clean lines; sexy but never over-the-top. "Kristin Davis dresses classic and up-to-date, and Charlotte dresses that way as well," says Patricia Field. "When we started out, we dressed her as a classic Americana girl. When she met Trey, that style became more pronounced, and then when she married and became a housewife, it became the more casual version of that."

Initially, Field wanted to go in a very different direction with Charlotte.

"My secret desire was to make Charlotte look more like Betty Page, a sweet, sexy look with a little bang. A woman who wanted a man to take care of her, like a Marilyn Monroe. Kristin has a tiny waist and sexy hips, and even though she sometimes feels it is what she wants to hide, I want to show it. I like to work with whatever special physical attributes the actresses have. It's good to recognize what they are and use them."

DRESS: *Tahari*
BAG: *Burberry*

DRESS: *Anna Molinari*

TOP: *Petite Bateau*
SKIRT: *Lacoste*

TOP: *Richard Tyler*
SKIRT: *Richard Tyler*
SHOES: *Manolo Blahnik*

DRESS: *Moschino*
BAG: *Fendi*

DRESS: *vintage*
SHOES: *Gucci*

Davis says she has become more confident in her own fashion choices. "Before I did the show," she confesses, "I had always thought fashion was a very rarified world I couldn't pull off. I knew a little about shoes, though. I remember Sarah Jessica came to my house one time and said, 'I'm so impressed by your shoes.' That's a big compliment coming from her. But in general I was intimidated by fashion. It's been a really great learning experience working with Pat."

Getting used to the high heels, Davis says, has been a learning experience in and of itself. She wore a high pair of Manolo Blahniks for "Politically Erect," the episode in which the girls went to a political fundraiser. "I was supposed to be on a quest for a man to marry and I headed off to talk to some men. I was looking at an extra across the room, and walking with determination, and my toe got stuck on the carpet and I fell! My earring got caught on the extra's sweater and I was bleeding and face-down on the floor. I wasn't that badly hurt, but it was all for the shoes."

Davis says she enjoys the opportunity to buy her clothes at the end of the season. She doesn't always buy her own character's, though. "Sometimes I buy some of Cynthia's clothes. I have some really great, chunky, big Miranda sweaters."

P: Laundry
RT: Agnès B.

DRESS: Blumarine
WATCH: Cartier

NIGHTGOWN: vintage

DRESS: David Gregory
BAG: Charles Jourdan

DRESS: Shoshana
BAG: Louis Vuitton

DRESS: Howard Wolf

Miranda

"Miranda's wardrobe is more dictated by her profession than any other character's," says Patricia Field. "Because she is a lawyer, it's very tailored. Cynthia's personal style is not so tailored, so we try to give her character a pop-ethnic look with mixed patterns and colors when she's not at work."

"I love the outfit I'm wearing when the dog is crying in the night and I pick up the dog and Steve isn't on the couch because he is sleeping at his new girlfriend's house," says Nixon. "It's a batik top and pants, a very expensive outfit, but Pat decided I could sleep in it."

Other faves for Nixon are the dress she wears in L.A. for the scene when the girls step out of the hotel for a moment; the outfit she wears to the Playboy Mansion; and the red suit she wears when telling Carrie she wants to help Steve find an apartment. Nixon enjoys her tailored suits but also likes Miranda's more casual outfits. "I think that it is a great relief when you see Miranda at home and she's wearing sweatpants and a T-shirt," says Nixon. "Miranda has a lot of masculine aspects, like sweatpants.

SUIT: *Barneys Co-op*
SHOES: *Michael Perry*
BAG: *vintage*

DRESS: *Jean Paul Gaultier*
BAG: *blue-beaded clutch*

SHIRT: *Tahari*
SKIRT: *Theory*
SHOES: *Prada*

BAG: *Chanel*

SUIT: *Tahari*
TOP: *Ultra Ozbek*

SUIT: *Taha...*
TOP: *Theo...*
BAG: *Furi...*

I would never wear them, but I think Miranda is either put together or she does not care at all."

Nixon also tries to incorporate some of her own clothing into the character. For example, she sometimes wears silver earrings that belonged to her grandmother. More than half of her own wardrobe consists of clothing from the show. "I love the way Miranda dresses. I love the way all the women dress. I just love having clothes in my closet."

The one area of fashion that doesn't intrigue Nixon at all is the shoes. "They are beautiful, but the idea of wearing those kinds of shoes in real life is just baffling to me. I made sure Miranda did not wear heels in the episodes in which she was pregnant. I said, 'There is no way.'"

TOP: *Bebe*
SKIRT: *Bebe*
SHOES: *Hogan*

SUIT: *Bebe*
BAG: *Desmo*

JACKET: *Ellen Tracy*
SKIRT: *Armani*
SHOES: *Michel Perry*

TOP: *DKNY*
PANTS: *DKNY*
BAG: *Rafe*

DRESS: *Mollie Parnis*

BAG: *Gucci*

tutu or not tutu?

The opening sequence of *Sex and the City* is a mini-episode itself. In it we have: New York (represented by the skyline and a New York City icon, a Metropolitan Transit Authority bus); Sarah Jessica Parker in a wild but quintessentially "Carrie" outfit, a tutu; and a story line in which Carrie is surprised and humiliated as a bus with her image goes through a puddle and splashes her. The sequence is comedic, iconic, and, thanks to its costume choice, highly controversial.

"The tutu was considered either the greatest success or the greatest failure of our show," says executive producer Michael Patrick King. "People either loved or hated it, and there was no way around it."

Once Darren Star and Pam Thomas, the title sequence director, came up with a concept, the next big decision was wardrobe. "This was going to be the opening shot that people would see every week," Patricia Field remembers, "so the wardrobe was important. Everyone wanted to know, 'What is she going to wear?'"

Field and Parker came up with the idea of Carrie wearing a tulle skirt—technically speaking, not a tutu. "I didn't want to have anything trendy," says Field, "since it was going to be used as the opening for each show. I knew it had to be great-looking and attention-grabbing, but I didn't want it to be of a certain season, because after a few years it would look tired." Field felt the tulle skirt was especially appropriate for Parker since the actress had been a ballerina when she was a girl.

Parker loved the tulle skirt, though she and Field were pretty much the only ones who did: "I felt it set the sequence up nicely, but it didn't give away the joke, the pie in the face. But nobody wanted me to wear it. Frankly, had I had my way, it would have even been a bigger silhouette of a tutu, rather than the tiered cupcake thing. I would have had a more classic, Degas-like, properly layered tutu because I think it would have been prettier."

On shooting day, the opinions about what Carrie should wear were so mixed that four different

dresses were brought to the set. One was a sky-blue Marc Jacobs slipdress with a netted dress over it. "It was really lovely," recalls Parker, "and it looked great against the film stock and the city, but it was fairly formfitting and it didn't move the same way." The shooting was complicated because it involved so much traffic control—on Fifth Avenue. "There weren't many runs we could do around the block with this bus splash," says Star, "so by the time we got it right with the tutu, we didn't have time to splash the blue dress." But since Star wanted some variety in costume, they shot another version with Carrie in the Marc Jacobs dress—without the splash. In it, she sees the bus, trips but doesn't fall, and keeps going.

"I always figured we could someday replace the tutu sequence with the other one," says Star, "and it could be our version of *The Dick Van Dyke Show.* In the first few seasons, he would trip over that ottoman when he was coming home, and later he learned to avoid it."

Today it is difficult to imagine a tutu-less opening. Although the World Trade Center was removed from the skyline sequence after September 11, 2001 (it used to appear next to Parker's name), the tutu has remained.

"The tutu is bizarre and the signature piece of the show," says King. He should know. The original is framed in glass in his *Sex and the City* office.

"All I have to do to meet the ideal man is give birth to him."
—MIRANDA HOBBES

MIRANDA HOBBES

PLAYED BY CYNTHIA NIXON

With her quick wit, pragmatism, and deeply held opinions, Miranda Hobbes represents the realist in all of us. A Harvard Law-educated lawyer, she is always the first of the four women to point out the sexual double standard. Her favorite coffee-shop topics are sexism, power, and hypocrisy, and she is utterly unafraid to say what she thinks.

Miranda's funniest moments usually contrast her overly defined sense of boundaries with a world that lets it all hang out. She dated a dirty talker, and then, after letting go of her inhibitions, said the one thing a woman should never say to a man in bed: "You love a finger up your ass." She withstood a phone-sexer who was having phone sex with other women; a guy who died the night of their date; and a guy who could only have sex in public places. Yet in each of these humiliating escapades, Miranda left perplexed but resilient.

Sharp as nails and hilariously sarcastic, Miranda was the most brittle of the women—until she met Steve Brady. It was the middle of Season Two, and she had just lamented to her friends, "If they're not married, they're gay, or burned from a divorce, or aliens from the planet 'Don't date me.'" But then, as if someone up above heard her plea, she went into a bar, ordered a glass of red wine, and met a curly-haired bartender.

Steve was as working-class and cuddly as she wasn't, and he adored her unashamedly, lovingly calling her "a real pisser." According to writer Jenny Bicks, who wrote the episode in which the two start dating, "Miranda is very much about order and logic and has trouble

when it comes to being emotionally available, whereas Steve is an open book of acceptance. That's hard for her, because she is so insecure." Though they complemented each other emotionally, other issues kept driving them apart—class differences, her pessimism, his childish qualities—and they broke up, twice.

In the middle of Season Four, Miranda faced some new obstacles. Her mother died, and Miranda allowed herself to accept the love of her friends. Soon after the funeral, she learned that Steve had testicular cancer. To convince him he was just as sexy with one testicle as two, she gave him a "mercy fuck," and got pregnant with his baby. And after agonizing over her options, she realized maybe there was no "right" time and decided to keep the child.

During her pregnancy, she was such a nontraditional expectant mother that she made us wonder if she'd made the right decision after all. For her baby shower, she insisted on fried chicken instead of crustless bread and nearly injured someone else's baby because she wasn't watching him closely enough. When she gave birth to a baby boy, she named him Brady Hobbes, combining Steve's name with hers, took the baby in her arms, and said, "I feel like there's a giraffe in the room."

Although Miranda can be harsh and sometimes judgmental, she has a cute, reluctant smile that creeps out whenever she finds herself charmed. And though it takes a lot to charm this woman of steel, underneath her hard exterior beats a soft, soulful heart.

BIO: The consummate New York actress, Cynthia Nixon has the unique distinction of having appeared in two Broadway plays at the same time—David Rabe's *Hurlyburly* and Tom Stoppard's *The Real Thing*—when she was only eighteen years old. Her other Broadway credits include *Angels in America*, *Indiscretions*, and *The Women*. Nixon made her film debut in *Little Darlings* in 1980, and has appeared in *Amadeus*, *The Pelican Brief*, *Marvin's Room*, and *The Out-of-Towners*. Her television work includes Wendy Wasserstein's *Kiss-Kiss, Dahlings!*, *Fifth of July*, and *The Murder of Mary Phagan*. Nixon and her boyfriend, Daniel Mozes, live on the Upper West Side with their young daughter. Nixon has been nominated for two Golden Globe awards for her portrayal of the acerbic Miranda Hobbes.

Cynthia Nixon

I WANT TO BE IN THIS THING When my agent sent me the script for the *Sex and the City* pilot, I was really excited by it. I thought, *I want to play any of these parts. I just want to be in this thing*—partly because it was shot in New York and also because it was very witty. They auditioned me a million times, and then I went in front of the network and didn't hear anything for a couple of months. My agent would call them and say, "What's happening?" They would say, "She's our first choice. We haven't found anybody we like better, but we are not ready to make an offer." I think my agent just wore them down because I was being offered other projects. She said, "You are about to lose her," and they cast me. I couldn't believe it, because it had been such a long road.

Before we did the pilot, I read Candace Bushnell's book, *Sex and the City,* and loved it. I found it really shocking and foreign. It gave you a bird's-eye view into the world of the wealthy and decadent—the amount of cash being thrown around, and all the casual sex and lost people. Our show is very different than her book, but the book gave our show legs because it has roots in something real.

BEING MIRANDA HOBBES I was excited about playing somebody who was so angry, bitter, and cynical because, having been a child actor with long blonde hair, I was always playing sweet, waiflike, hippie characters. It was nice to grow out of that. Miranda is less angry than she used to be, partly because we know her better and have gotten to see what's underneath. And Steve has mellowed her. He's been an easygoing presence in her life, and her girlfriends have helped her to open up.

Miranda was very career-minded in terms of college and law school and in getting ahead in her firm. When she arrived professionally, it made her look around and say, "This is not all there is." She realized she wanted more gentleness and humanity in her life. Miranda is in the most male-dominated profession of the four women. She feels she is making a place for women where there wasn't a place before. Sarah Jessica and I used to say that Carrie and Miranda must have gone to college together, because where else would they have met? You can imagine how the other three women met each other, but where would they have met Miranda?

I think Carrie is Miranda's best friend. The other three women would not be together if they didn't have Carrie in common. In Season Four, Miranda runs into Charlotte on the street and confronts her about what a hard time she's giving her about wanting to have an abortion, and that's the first time Kristin and I ever had a scene alone. Kim and I have little bits together because Miranda and Samantha line up more naturally. Samantha and Miranda are the more masculine characters, and Carrie and Charlotte are the more feminine.

It was exciting to do the fight scene with Carrie about Big at the end of the third season. You don't want it to be too safe and too lovey-dovey. These women love and support each other unconditionally, but they also have very different points of view and are bound to clash. Sometimes their philosophies can run really deep, and when your philosophy is threatened, it can make you very impassioned in your fight for it.

SEX SCENES I had never done sex scenes before this show, but they're not too bad. Nudity to me is not such a big deal. I breast-fed on the subway, so the idea of someone seeing my breast is nonimportant. I'm more self-conscious about areas below the waist. I like nudity when it seems like part of the scene and feels like real people. When it seems crazy and gratuitous, I'm less fond of it.

Filming a sex scene is not sexy. We cut right to the chase with the director about how they're going to be shot. We have special wardrobe items to make it look like we're naked. Sometimes we wear G-strings, but if it's a scene in which a man is seen from behind, he can't wear a G-string, so this flesh-colored cloth covering is taped to the front. Sarah Jessica and Kristin sometimes wear bras that cover the front and are taped to the sides so there is a bare back. In most of my sex scenes, I wear big boxer shorts.

Most of the guys who come on have never done a sex scene before. I just try to make them feel comfortable. Even when it seems real, it feels very fake because we don't show an entire lovemaking session. It's quiet, and then you hear "Action," and all of a sudden you start screaming. For an actor that feels pretty phony.

THE WOMEN *Sex and the City* is about how important friendships are when you're not married and don't have a family. It's a gay thing, and a single-person thing, where your friends are your family. I was in the play *The Women,* in which there's this age-old idea that women are competitive with one another, that women consider men to be the most important and will do anything to get a man and keep that man happy, and whatever females are in your life can fall by the wayside. I've never found that to be true, personally. I like to have a guy in my life, but my mother and my girlfriends are very important. Maybe when women weren't allowed to be competitive in the workplace or in the world in general, the only place in which they could be competitive was in looks, clothes, or men.

The show has made singlehood look more fun. Whether or not these women end up getting married, marriage is not the only measure of their lives. The show has moments that make you really pleased to be a woman or to be single, and then it has moments that make you really sad to be both of those things.

Miranda on Men & Marriage

In fifty years men are going to be obsolete, anyway.
Already you can't talk to them.
You don't need 'em to have kids with.
You don't even need them to have sex with anymore.

My right ovary has given up hope that I will ever
get married and have kids. It's like working on a case
that you know is going to settle out of court.
Why bother?

A thirty-four-year-old guy with no money
and no place to live, because he's single,
he's a catch. But a thirty-four-year-old woman
with a job and a great home,
because she's single, is considered tragic.

Reasonable doubt in a courtroom
gets you off for murder. In an engagement,
it makes you feel like a bad person.

I was once with a guy the size of one of those
miniature-golf pencils. I couldn't tell if he was trying
to fuck me or erase me.

Oral sex is like God's gift to women. You can get off
without worrying about getting pregnant.

I know how to please a man. You just give away
most of your power.

Married people are the enemy.

If the first season was predicated on fantastical comedic situations and the second on deeper emotional story lines, the third season mastered the art of blending the two.

In episode after episode, funny, ribald sex scenes were intercut with moving emotional confrontations. A perfect example was "Easy Come, Easy Go," in which Carrie reunited with Mr. Big and Samantha shot "funky spunk" into the popular lexicon. As the writing became more polished and layered, the production team upped the ante, too. The season's most memorable locations included the church in which Charlotte was married, the Staten Island Ferry, and the Playboy Mansion in Los Angeles. A series of scrumptious guest stars added to the excitement: Vince Vaughn, Sarah Michelle Gellar, Donovan Leitch, Alanis Morissette, and the beloved Frances Sternhagen (who played Trey's mother, Bunny).

In the drama department, Carrie showed the most character movement: she met and fell in love with Aidan, cheated on him with Big in the Stanhope hotel, lost Aidan's dog, lied to him about her cheating, eventually told him the truth, and wound up with a broken heart. Charlotte met her dream man, Trey, and married him the morning after she discovered he was impotent. She forced him to deal with their sexual problems and asked him to love her for who she was. Miranda reunited with Steve, confronted his skid marks and her own fear of turning into "Mean Mommy," and realized they just couldn't make it work. And Samantha, the only one of the girls without a steady, revealed something emotionally painful, too: that she was older than her girlfriends. As the women ventured into foreign emotional terrain, they were forced to examine their own patterns for the first time and take responsibility for their own actions.

In the final episode, Carrie and Big met for lunch in Central Park and accidentally fell into a lake. This tumble, followed by a sweetly moving conversation in Big's bedroom between these two warriors of love, was an example of the show at its best. *Sex and the City* that third year was a series about leaping and looking.

*the L.A. vacay, the new boy named Trey, the Big that's in the way, the ex who wants to stay, one crazy wedding day

WHERE THERE'S SMOKE . . .

WRITTEN AND DIRECTED BY *michael patrick king*

"Do women just want to be rescued?"
The girls venture across the river to Staten Island for the Fire Department of New York's Annual Calendar Competition, where Samantha meets a fiery firefighter and Carrie meets Bill Kelley, a charismatic local politician. After Steve escorts Miranda home from her laser eye surgery, she learns that being rescued isn't always a sign of weakness; Charlotte meets a white knight who turns out to be . . . a white nightmare.

MICHAEL PATRICK KING (EXECUTIVE PRODUCER)**:**

I knew there was a real fireman-calendar competition and I thought it was a great story. Jen McNamara, the casting director, and I got a copy of the fireman calendar, and I wrote the character of a dumb fireman who was really hot but really sweet. Mike Lombardi, a real fireman, came in to audition. He had a voice that was very flat. The minute he opened his mouth, I thought, *That's exactly right*. For legal reasons we couldn't have any New York Fire Department clothes on when he was doing the sex scene, so he had to be completely naked.

KRISTIN DAVIS (CHARLOTTE)**:**

The reaction to that line, "I've been dating since I was fifteen. I'm exhausted. Where is he?" continues to amaze me. People tell me it's their favorite line of the whole series. I remember thinking that I hadn't done it the way I wanted to, which is generally how it works. I did not expect so many people to connect to it the way they did.

SEX and the CITY
★ ★ ★ ★ ★
By Carrie Bradshaw

To Pee or Not to Pee, That Is the Question

'hat exactly makes an inno-
'tle sexual perversion? Is
'esting little something
"wants" you to do
'n and quirky,
'» "need"

do something in bed with
boyfriend that I could
manage alone in a p''
room. So maybe h
sider closing '
could d'''

POLITICALLY ERECT

WRITTEN BY *darren star*
DIRECTED BY *michael patrick king*

"Can there be sex without politics?"
Charlotte throws a used-date party; Steve asks Miranda to be monogamous; Samantha meets a Tiny Tim who's great in bed but shops in the Bloomingdale's boys department; Carrie has to decide whether to indulge her politician when he reveals his desire to be "showered" with affection.

DARREN STAR (CREATOR)**:**

The idea of using a politician who had a sexual fetish that came into conflict with Carrie's column was interesting to me. I started with that notion of the politician. It was the idea of hypocrisy, politics, and judgments that people make about one another. Here was a guy who had this weird fetish, and suddenly he was trying to turn the tables on Carrie. But when she wrote that column about it, she got the last laugh.

CARRIE: *Are you guys seriously advocating that I do this?* **SAMANTHA:** *Why not? He's a great-looking, rich political prince.*
CARRIE: *Oh sure, it's practically a fairy tale. The princess and the pee.*

3

ATTACK OF THE FIVE-FOOT-TEN-INCH WOMAN

WRITTEN BY *cindy chupack* DIRECTED BY *pam thomas*

"Are there women in New York who are just there to make us feel bad about ourselves?"

Carrie gets thrown for a loop when she discovers in the *New York Times* Style section that Mr. Big and Natasha have tied the knot; Samantha takes the girls out for a day at a spa but can't get her masseur to offer special treatment, while Charlotte has trouble getting naked in the steam room; Miranda's new housekeeper attempts to replace Miranda's vibrator with a Virgin Mary.

BEHIND-THE-SCENES TIDBIT:

In the original ending of the script, Miranda's cleaning lady arranged the condoms on a plate with the Blessed Virgin in the middle. But both HBO and the producers felt that was going too far, so they took the Virgin out and kept the condoms.

4

BOY, GIRL, BOY, GIRL

WRITTEN BY *jenny bicks*
DIRECTED BY *pam thomas*

"If we can take the best of the other sex and make it our own, has the opposite sex become obsolete?"

Charlotte meets a photographer who wants her to pose for him—as a man; Carrie's new boy toy is bi; Samantha is attracted to her new assistant, which creates problems at work; Steve tells Miranda she's like the guy sometimes.

MICHAEL PATRICK KING:

Sarah Jessica lives the show so deeply. The loft party she goes to and gets kissed by Alanis Morissette was one of those Broome Street lofts, five staircases up. Carrie leaves the loft at four in the morning and is about to go down one flight of stairs and then down and down and down. And before she comes around the corner to go down the next flight, Sarah Jessica, not as Sarah Jessica but as Carrie, turns to check to make sure no one is there to kill her. It's very subtle, but it is just what a New Yorker would do.

5

NO IFS, ANDS, OR BUTTS

WRITTEN BY *michael patrick king*
DIRECTED BY *nicole holofcener*

"In relationships, what are the deal breakers?"

Charlotte dates a man who kisses like a Great Dane; Carrie meets a furniture designer named Aidan who says he can't date a smoker; Samantha goes out with Chivon, a sexy African-American, but gets in trouble when she meets his sister; Steve tells Miranda she needs to be more supportive.

JOE COLLINS (FIRST ASSISTANT CAMERA)**:**

The scene when Stanford jumps on the guy with the doll collection was Willie Garson's first gay love scene. The scene is all lit and ready to go, we bring the actors in, and the director calls "Action." They say their lines, Willie jumps on the guy, they're rolling all over the bed, he gets kicked out, and the director says, "Cut on rehearsal." Willie was in shock. He says, "You got to be kidding me. I've been rolling around with this guy and you didn't have film in the camera?"

6

ARE WE SLUTS?

WRITTEN BY *cindy chupack*
DIRECTED BY *nicole holofcener*

"Are we simply romantically challenged or are we sluts?"

Carrie wonders why Aidan doesn't want to have sex with her; Charlotte has sex with a guy who has to insult her to achieve orgasm; Miranda gets chlamydia and has to call all her ex-lovers to let them know they may be infected; Samantha moves after her neighbors ostracize her for being too promiscuous.

CINDY CHUPACK (CO-EXECUTIVE PRODUCER)**:**

I based the Miranda story on a good friend of mine who got chlamydia and had to call the guys she slept with. While I was working on the episode, I saw my friend in L.A. driving to work. We just happened to be near each other at a light and I rolled down the window and yelled over, "Now did you actually have to *call* them when you had chlamydia?" She said, "Can we talk about this later?"

AIDAN: *I'm going to get going. But that doesn't make us friends, because I'll be thinking about you naked.*

DRAMA QUEENS

WRITTEN BY *darren star*
DIRECTED BY *allison anders*

**"Do we need drama
to make a relationship work?"**

Carrie encounters Big at the opera; Charlotte falls down on the street and meets Dr. Trey MacDougal; Miranda does Steve's wash and realizes she's dating "Skid-Marks Guy"; Samantha dates a doctor and becomes a Viagra junkie.

KRISTIN DAVIS:

It was difficult for me to do the lines where Charlotte talks about the book that's supposed to teach women how to find husbands. I don't believe in that *Rules* kind of thing, and I think it's a toxic message to be putting out there in the world. But once the writers said, "We're going to build it up that you are looking at marriage like a business, and then it's going to blow up in your face," I was all right with it. When a person gets fixated on one goal, it never works.

Marriage INC.

How to Apply Successful Business Strategies to Finding a Husband

by

SABRINA WRIGHT-GILLIAR

THE BIG TIME

WRITTEN BY *jenny bicks*
DIRECTED BY *allison anders*

"Is timing everything?"

In an effort to revirginize herself, Charlotte has vowed not to have sex with Trey until they marry; Miranda, tired of mothering Steve, ends the relationship; Samantha worries she's day-old bread; Big shows up at Carrie's door and confesses he can't stop thinking about her.

CHRIS NOTH (MR. BIG)**:**

In the scene where I run up to Carrie's apartment and knock on the door, I added the line "I'm so fucked up." I think everyone's been at that place where you're really desperately humiliated and you still do it. They kept it, and I was really happy. But the show is written so precisely and so well that for the most part, there's not much ad-libbing.

EASY COME, EASY GO

WRITTEN BY *michael patrick king*
DIRECTED BY *charles mcdougall*

"When it comes to relationships, is it smarter to follow your heart or your head?"

Miranda lets Steve squat on her couch and has second thoughts about their breakup; Charlotte asks Trey to marry her, and he says, "Alrighty"; Samantha's latest lover has "funky spunk"; Carrie and Mr. Big reunite in the Stanhope hotel, and he tells her he loves her without using the word "fucking" as a modifier.

KIM CATTRALL (SAMANTHA)**:**

All the guys have what they call a "KC cup" on during sex scenes. Those are my initials. It's for everybody's comfort level. Bobby Cannavale, who played Adam Ball, the funky spunk guy, is a real pro and loves women. The shot where he's standing up was his idea. I'm not really near him, I'm over to the side. What you see is basically just my expression when I turn away. I felt like I was next to a leg. But it was an excellent cheat because when I see it—and I know what was going on—I think, *My God, that looks authentic.*

ALL OR NOTHING

WRITTEN BY *jenny bicks*
DIRECTED BY *charles mcdougall*

"Can we have it all?"

Carrie confesses her affair to Samantha, who refuses to judge her; Samantha gets the flu and can't find a man to take care of her; Trey gives his princess a prenup (pictured here), which Miranda reviews for Charlotte; Miranda has phone sex with a guy who is dirty-talking other women.

SARAH JESSICA PARKER (CARRIE)**:**

We thought long and hard about Carrie having that affair. It was discussed and discussed. To the very end, HBO was chewing its fingers off about losing Aidan, bringing him back, and then losing him again. Carrie's relationship with Big was already so complicated. It's not like she just met this man on the street and didn't know he was married. It's a very conscious adult decision to make, and you have to deal with the consequences. HBO was worried about how to deal with it responsibly and how to make sure that Carrie's friends were real with her about it, and that Carrie would be able to recover.

AIDAN: *I don't want to be paranoid here, but you took Pete for a walk, and we both know you are not big on the dog-walking thing.*
And I smell something. Are you cheating? I can smell the smoke on you. **CARRIE:** *Oh.*

94

11

RUNNING WITH
SCISSORS

WRITTEN BY *michael patrick king*
DIRECTED BY *dennis erdman*

"When you crawl in bed
with someone, is sex ever safe?"

Miranda is harassed by a hoagie; Samantha meets a guy who's ready to strap her into a sex swing but insists she get an HIV test first; Charlotte hires a stylist to help her pick out her wedding dress; Carrie relapses with Big in his conjugal bed—and then has a run-in with Natasha.

MICHAEL PATRICK KING:

Once I was going through Macy's at Christmastime, and there was a guy in a puppet show. You couldn't see his face, but he was doing puppets and walking around. I was with my friend John, and John said, "Oh, grow up," and from inside, the guy said, "Fuck you." His voice changed. Later I saw a guy dressed up as a sandwich on the street and thought, *"Eat me." That would be funny.*

12

DON'T ASK,
DON'T TELL

WRITTEN BY *cindy chupack*
DIRECTED BY *dan algrant*

"In a relationship, is honesty really
the best policy?"

Miranda pretends to be a stewardess to make a man more interested; Charlotte goes to Trey's the night before the wedding and learns that there's a downside to postponing sex; Samantha has an affair with Trey's Hot Scot cousin; Carrie confesses her affair to Aidan, who breaks up with her.

CINDY CHUPACK:

I had read an article in the *New York Times* about speed dating, so I came up with the Miranda story. But the idea of her lying and saying she is a stewardess is something I relate to. Jenny Bicks and I always joke that even though we are very successful TV comedy writers, it does us no good. The most nebbishy guy comedy writer can end up with a gorgeous model woman because he writes for *Seinfeld*, and we are here on the hottest show, and it doesn't seem to count for anything with men.

CHARLOTTE: *I just should have slept with him on the first date.* CARRIE: *Um . . . maybe he jerked off right before you got there and he was just too embarrassed to tell ya. Okay?* CHARLOTTE: *I do love him.* CARRIE: *And he loves you.* CHARLOTTE: *Maybe he did jerk off.*

95

13

ESCAPE FROM NEW YORK

WRITTEN BY *becky hartman edwards & michael patrick king*
DIRECTED BY *john david coles*

"No matter how far you travel or how much you run from it . . . can you ever really escape your past?"

In a spur-of-the-moment jaunt, the girls, sans Charlotte, head to LA-LA-land. Samantha dates a dildo model; Matthew McConaughey hits on Carrie; Miranda gets in touch with her inner vamp when she rides a mechanical bull; back in NY, Charlotte does an experiment to get to the bottom of Trey's sexual performance.

MICHAEL PATRICK KING:

I wrote the part of the movie star for Alec Baldwin, and he didn't want to do it. His name was on the script, so we took his name off and put "movie star." We heard George Clooney was interested, but he couldn't do it. At this point we were in Hollywood, three days away from shooting, and we didn't have a star. The script was sent to Warren Beatty, and everyone was telling us he was interested. One night we got invited to this *New York Times* political party and saw Warren Beatty and Annette Bening. Jenny went up to him, introduced herself, and said, "We'd love you to do our show." He said, "Oh yeah, I got the script." She introduced me, he looked at me and said, "How many Hollywood movie stars did you have to change the name of this guy to before you gave me the script?" I said, "Nine, but you're the very first choice!" He drove away in his car and said, "Never took it seriously."

14

SEX AND ANOTHER CITY

WRITTEN BY *jenny bicks*
DIRECTED BY *john david coles*

"When it comes to bags, men, and cities, is it really what's outside that counts?"

Miranda gets together with Lew, an old New York friend, who has turned from pissed to placid; Carrie dates a man she thinks is an agent (Vince Vaughn) but who turns out to be a house sitter to the stars; Charlotte hops a plane to L.A. and admits to the girls that she and Trey are not having sex; Samantha meets Hugh Hefner and gets her fake Fendi stolen at a Playboy Mansion party.

SARAH JESSICA PARKER:

The one story the writers took from my life was when I had a bikini wax that went further than I had anticipated. That's it. But I even told them, "You have got to do this story, because I was robbed." I didn't know what was happening. I was freezing and naked, and I was so flipped out by it.

DARREN STAR:

Shooting at the Playboy Mansion was a hoot. Hugh Hefner would always come to the *Sex and the City* parties. He was our original fan. And that's not an easy place to shoot. Not many people get to go film there. But I thought it was too perfect to see the girls in the Playboy Mansion.

TREY: *Charlotte, what are you getting at?* CHARLOTTE: *Well, just that, well, we've tried everything else, and we still . . . you haven't . . . in my . . . ever.*

15

HOT CHILD IN THE CITY

WRITTEN BY *allan heinberg*
DIRECTED BY *michael spiller*

"Are we thirty-four going on thirteen?"
When Samantha is hired as the publicist for an A-list Bat Mitzvah, she starts to wonder whether there's any difference between women and girls; Miranda's new braces make her feel like a teenager; Charlotte and Trey see a sex therapist and learn to name their privates; Carrie dates a comic-book artist who still lives with his parents.

When we did the scene with Trey masturbating in the bathroom, all the guys on the crew turned into thirteen-year-old boys. Everyone was acting out, being very boisterous, and they had the dirty magazine, which was horrific. I came around the corner, and all the guys had it open to this picture, which was the biggest close-up I've ever seen of a woman's organs. I screamed, turned around, and left. Then we got ready to do the scene, and someone—I never found out who— gave Kyle a dildo. When I came in the door for the scene, he was holding it in place. I didn't have a good reaction.

16

FRENEMIES

WRITTEN BY *jenny bicks*
DIRECTED BY *michael spiller*

"Are we getting wiser, or just older?"
Miranda gets stood up by a guy who she later discovers has died; Carrie teaches a seminar on singlehood at the Learning Annex; Charlotte and Trey try to resolve their bedroom problems; Samantha gets out-Samantha-ed.

I love the story line where Charlotte tells Trey she loves him but she's sexual, and I wanted to do it well. Michael Spiller, the director, said he didn't need to actually show anything to get it done. The camera was going to be far away. I come out of the bathroom in the nightgown and this little G-string and high heels. We did it maybe three times, and the last time was the best. Michael came up and said, "God, that was great." And Joe Collins came up and said, "Um, I'm not sure if we should say this, but when you moved a little, I might have gotten a little nipple action." I thought, *Oh no*. But I couldn't imagine doing it again, so I didn't. It was a difficult weekend when that show aired because I got so many phone calls about it. But many of them were compliments from my girlfriends who know how hard a scene like that would be for me to do.

CHARLOTTE: *Look at me. This is me. I'm not a Madonna, and I'm not a whore. I'm your wife . . . and I'm sexual, and I love you.*

NATASHA: *Yes, I'm sorry about it all. I'm sorry that he moved to Paris and fell in love with me, I'm sorry that we ever got married, I'm sorry he cheated on me with you, and I'm sorry that I pretended to ignore it for as long as I did. I'm sorry I found you in my apartment, fell down the stairs, and broke my tooth. I'm very sorry that after much painful dental surgery, this tooth is still a different color than this tooth. Finally, I'm very sorry that you felt the need to come down here. Now not only have you ruined my marriage, you've ruined my lunch.*

WHAT GOES AROUND COMES AROUND

WRITTEN BY *darren star* DIRECTED BY *allen coulter*

"Is there such a thing as relationship karma?"

Carrie gets mugged for her Manolos—then learns that Natasha has left Big; Samantha gets calls for a guy named Sam Jones and decides to bed her namesake; Miranda dates the gorgeous detective on Carrie's case—only to find that she's so intimidated by his looks she has to get drunk to get through the date. Charlotte kisses Trey's gardener, and when Trey doesn't get jealous, she suggests they separate.

DARREN STAR:

I wanted people to be angry at Carrie, to have the character they love do something wrong. Like real people, she sullies herself and makes errors in judgment and does things that she can't ever really make right. It makes her more relatable, like when she's trying to apologize to Big's wife, and it's impossible. She can't. She's not going to be forgiven.

COCK A DOODLE DO!

WRITTEN BY *michael patrick king*
DIRECTED BY *allen coulter*

"Is it us?"

Samantha has a run-in with the transsexual prostitutes outside her apartment, whose late-night cackling is keeping her awake at night; Miranda and Carrie have a fight about their relationships with men; Big and Carrie decide they're a good idea on paper but not meant to be; Charlotte gets a late-night visit from Trey, who, turned on by the prospect of losing her, manages to keep the wind in his Schooner's sails.

SARAH JESSICA PARKER:

Before we shot the scene at the pond in Central Park, they dredged it and took out tons of garbage. We practiced the scene and did it in one take. We had multiple cameras set up, and if you look at that scene, you see that both of us are terrified. There were no cuts, so we went from our close-ups to falling. I actually cut my foot at the bottom and they had to give me a tetanus shot right afterward.

MAKING *Sex and the City*

Though critics and fans point to the acting and writing as *Sex and the City*'s keys to success, others watch it simply because it *looks* so darn good. Sure, it helps to have four knockout ladies as the leads, but *two hundred and fifty* experienced, perfectionist professionals bust their booties each week to ensure that the casting, sets, locations, set decoration, costumes, props, lighting, camera, direction, editing, music, and sound meet the same high standards as the performances themselves.

The process starts with the writers, who begin their work in November, and those involved in the final mix work until the final episodes air, sometimes as late as September. Without the commitment, genius, and hard work of the pre-production, production, and post-production crews, *Sex and the City* would, quite simply, not exist. The process of preparing each episode for broadcast is involved and exhausting but also exceedingly fun. As set decorator Karin Wiesel puts it, "Most of the crew have been there since the first year, which is great. There's a certain language that we all speak. We all know how everyone works and exactly what to expect from each other."

JOHN MELFI, CO-EXECUTIVE PRODUCER

John Melfi describes himself as the "mom and pop" of *Sex and the City*. He is the hands-on producer who is responsible for coordinating all the different departments and ensuring that the show gets made every week. "There's that saying that you can have a great job, a great apartment, a great relationship, but only two of the three at the same time," says Melfi. "The producer's version of that is that you can have something done good and fast, fast and cheap, or good and cheap, but only two of the three at the same time."

pre-production

Months before the show goes into production, the writing staff is already hard at work developing story ideas and writing the scripts, which will eventually inform how given scenes must look, feel, and work in rhythm with each other.

Two weeks before shooting is set to start, the pre-production, or prep, phase begins. About three days into prep, the actors, producers, writers, and director gather for the "table read" to read through the scripts and determine how well each scene is working.

Because 40 percent of the show is shot on location, location scouting, led by production designer Jeremy Conway and the locations department (helmed by Seth Burch the first four seasons), is a crucial element of prep.

Jeremy Conway is also responsible for designing and building the sets. For both built sets and off-site locations, the set decorator, Karin Wiesel, is responsible for dressing all the sets—selecting the appropriate bedding, table settings, furniture, and wallpaper.

As set building and decoration are underway, costume designer Patricia Field and her team are busy gathering potential costumes for each scene and ensuring that the actresses are comfortable in them.

There's a saying that filmmaking is 90 percent casting, and many on the set of *Sex and the City* would agree. Casting director Jennifer McNamara and her associate Camille Hickman audition actors at Silvercup Studios for every speaking role until they find the perfect people.

The property department, run by Sabrina Wright, is responsible for finding or creating any item that an actor interacts with—a Rabbit, a bus, a cow, a cigarette, an invitation, a baby rattle.

production

CO-PRODUCER

The production stage, spearheaded by Jane Raab, is the period in which the shows are actually filmed. Raab supervises the day-to-day responsibilities of production, including crew hiring, equipment rental, and scheduling.

MAKEUP

The hair and makeup trailer is where the actresses go before shooting to run lines, listen to show tunes, and kick back with the eight hair and makeup artists.

BLOCKING

Before each scene is shot, the director "blocks," or stages, the scene. The writers watch a rehearsal to see how it looks, answer questions the actors and director might have, and make final adjustments to the dialogue.

STAND-INS

While lighting each scene properly, the crew uses stand-ins for each of the actresses, who are the same approximate height and coloring as Sarah Jessica Parker, Kim Cattrall, Kristin Davis, and Cynthia Nixon.

DIRECTING

In addition to Darren Star and Michael Patrick King, who have directed numerous episodes, the show uses many directors over the course of a season, and since shows are shot two scripts at a time, directors are hired for two shows at once.

SHOOTING

Two directors of photography (DPs) rotate responsibility—Michael Spiller, who has also directed several episodes, and John Thomas. The shooting days can often run fourteen hours or longer. "*Sex and the City* is unusual in that we do a lot of night shoots," points out creative consultant Amy B. Harris.

DAILIES

Every day the producers and writers watch the dailies (all the footage shot the day before) to make sure the show is coming to life in the way they had envisioned, and that the director is getting all the necessary shots.

CHAT-AND-CHEW

The longest scenes to shoot are often those in the coffee shop, because they involve all four actresses. In these scenes (called "chat-and-chews") the director must shoot not only master shots but close-ups of each of the actresses, which calls for shooting the scenes dozens of times.

post-production

The post-production stage is when the episodes are actually put together, in sequence, in a format that's fast, fresh, funny, and beautiful. Antonia Ellis supervises postproduction and is responsible for budgeting, hiring, and scheduling.

As soon as a scene is shot, the film goes straight to the editing room, where editors Michael Berenbaum and Wendey Stanzler begin cutting the episode together. This process is essential to creating the show's sense of comedy and drama—the two elements that keep people watching.

One important element of editing is continuity—ensuring that a purse or Cosmo glass does not magically switch from a right hand into a left between shots. "With the dailies we get, we can't lose," says Stanzler. "The actresses understand the filmmaking process and know that we can do anything we want with any of the performances because they all match."

"We never use music that spells out what the scene is about," says Lieberstein. "We look for the music that rhythmically is in gear with the people and the conversation. The overall feeling of the song can give a scene life and energy, which helps the jokes play well."

Since each show features one or more "think-and-types," when Carrie is musing and writing at her computer, Lieberstein and his colleagues score these scenes in a lively way. "Scoring those scenes can be difficult," he says, "because we are scoring Carrie thinking alone to herself, but we're also trying to score the question."

Once the director's cut is completed, the executive producer makes his cut. He may feel a certain scene is gratuitous or inappropriate for airing, or that an extra voiceover is necessary to clarify an event such as a breakup.

Parker is involved throughout the process, watching each of the cuts and notifying the executive producer when she feels strongly about something. "If something really bothers her, we'll change it," says Stanzler.

The final cut is HBO's, in which original programming executives give notes such as, "Was there a different performance for this shot?" Many times, however, there are no notes at all.

CO-PRODUCER

EDITING

CONTINUITY

SCORING

THINK & TYPE

APPROVALS

"Ladies, can we cut the cake and get out of here? I have a three-way to go to."
—SAMANTHA JONES

SAMANTHA JONES

PLAYED BY KIM CATTRALL

Whether you love Samantha or are appalled by her, the one thing you cannot do is ignore her. The wildest of the four friends, Samantha is the show's try-anything girl ("I'm a tri-sexual. I'll try anything once"). Over the course of the first four seasons, she has slept with thirty-eight men, two women (including herself), and numerous vibrators. She's come face-to-face with female ejaculation, cow's milk, and funky spunk. She has tried celibacy, lesbianism, sex swings, and yoga.

Her many beaus are a gorgeous mosaic of Manhattan men. She has dated men with servants, men who wrestle, a septuagenarian, and a college student. A fireman, a farmer, a baby talker. One beau was too big, while another was too small. She has tried marijuana, Viagra, and, after taking Ecstasy, was even able to say the unthinkable: "I'm in love with you!"

She's randy, opinionated, and adventure-some; there is no sexual act she will not try, no kink she won't indulge. She is self-made (she even fired her own assistant so she could sleep with him), self-protective, and sees monogamy as a disease she'd rather not catch.

Despite Samantha's predilection for fast, emotion-free sex, each season she has had a lover for whom she cared deeply. She met the first, James, at the end of the first season in a jazz club. He was loving and accommodating, but, unfortunately, had a penis the size of a pencil eraser. In Season Two Samantha got back in touch with an ex, Dominic, who had broken her heart. She

hoped to get revenge, but he wound up leaving her first—and she sobbed, "Stop beating me to the punch!" In the beginning of Season Four, she got embroiled with a lesbian artist named Maria, and after deciding relationships with women involved too much talking, she ended it—but not before a fabulous final night with a strap-on.

Later in the fourth season Samantha met her match, a suave hotelier and new client, Richard Wright. The two were partners in crime: they joined the mile-high club together, led independent lives, and refused to conform to the expectations of polite society. And then one night Richard invited her to his rooftop for a midnight swim, and Samantha realized she possessed something she didn't want to acknowledge: vulnerability. She agreed to become monogamous and gave Richard a painting of three hearts. And then, just as she was opening herself up to him, she discovered him in a compromising position with another woman. Furious, she smashed the painting and shouted, "Now your heart's broken, too!"

It was clear that although Samantha's outer warrior would never die, she had discovered her softer core. After years of living for sex, Samantha had learned that she wanted love, too. But until she found the right man, we hoped she would return to the decadence and sin for which we adored her. Because, as Ms. Jones herself put it, "I don't believe in the Democratic Party or the Republican Party. I just believe in parties."

BIO: Born in Liverpool, England, and raised on Vancouver Island in British Columbia, Canada, Cattrall moved to New York City on her own at age sixteen to attend the American Academy of Dramatic Arts. Her many blockbuster films include *Police Academy, Porky's, Mannequin, Masquerade, Star Trek VI: The Undiscovered Country, Big Trouble in Little China,* and *Bonfire of the Vanities.* Her performance as Jamie in the independent feature *Live Nude Girls* earned her rave reviews at film festivals; she also had a cameo appearance in the thriller *15 Minutes.* Onstage she has appeared in critically acclaimed productions of *A View from the Bridge, Three Sisters, Miss Julie,* and *Wild Honey.* She starred in the TNT adaptation of Wendy Wasserstein's Pulitzer Prize-winning play, *The Heidi Chronicles,* and in Oliver Stone's miniseries *Wild Palms* for ABC. She has also written a book with her husband, Mark Levinson, called *Satisfaction: The Art of the Female Orgasm.* Cattrall has been nominated for two Golden Globes and two Emmys for her portrayal of Samantha.

Kim Cattrall

DREAM ON I got a call from my agent asking me to read the pilot script, and I passed on it. Even though the show was on HBO and I had done an episode of *Dream On* that was really fun, I still thought the show wasn't for me. They came back to me and said, "We have Sarah Jessica involved, and it's going to shoot in New York." New York was my first home away from home, so it piqued my interest, but I didn't want to uproot myself. I had a lovely home in Los Angeles and had been there twenty-two years.

But I agreed to have lunch with Darren Star, and he was so accessible and approachable. His partner, Dennis Erdman, who was an old friend of mine, was there, and so was Candace Bushnell. I thought she was funny, outrageous, and very New York, which made me think the show could have some authenticity. But after the lunch I went home, thought about it, and said to myself, *I don't think so.*

The most difficult thing for an actor to do is to commit six years of your life, especially when you're in your forties. I was doing independent films and theater and feeling very satisfied. And I didn't know where the characters were going to go. It was a lot for me to gamble on.

They hired another actress, and I got a call from Dennis on a Sunday morning. He used to be head of casting at NBC, and he said, "I think this is your role. Nobody is going to play it the way you're going to play it, and I feel this so innately. I am wondering if there is any way you and Darren can sit down on Monday. They start in three weeks and it doesn't work with the other actress the way it's going to work with you."

I was overwhelmed that Dennis felt strongly enough to call me and keep pursuing it. I had a very uneasy night, tossing and turning and thinking, *What am I going to do?* That Monday I had lunch with Darren and said, "These are my concerns. This is what I don't want to be doing, and this is what I do want to be doing. How can you assure me that that's going to happen?"

He said, "I can't, but I think we have something really special. We're bringing new writers in, we're going to finesse it, and we're open to what you have to say." That was very important to me. There was something about Darren being so honest with me. His honesty made me think I had enough to go on, and I went to HBO later that day. They paid the other actress her sum and hired me.

JONES VERSUS CATTRALL When I was single, it took me a lot longer to get over any kind of intimate relationship than it does for Samantha. The interesting thing about watching Samantha change and grow is that you see that she's not as laissez-faire as she likes to think she is, either. I never really slept around. I didn't have—I don't know if anyone has—the voracious appetite that Samantha does.

I love my girlfriends like Samantha does. I feel really great with women, and my love for my mom was a great start in my life. I'm different from Samantha in that I don't need to be the life of the party. I like my down time, and I like to get away from the craziness of New York City and *Sex and the City.* I like to lay low, recoup and regroup, and have time for my husband and myself.

Samantha is street-smart. I imagine that she was an assistant to somebody like [famed public relations exec] Peggy Siegel and learned things the hard way. I think she might have gone to college and taken business or communications classes, but she never went to one of those Ivy League bullshit schools. She reads people and circumstances. I think she's the oldest in her family and was the trailblazer. She had a strong relationship with her father and her mother, but she was also the one that broke away. There's a feeling with her that she's always had to pay her own way.

WOMEN, SEX, AND COMEDY

All of us are pioneers as comedians with this material. Other than Mae West and Madeleine Kahn, who was amazing, this is territory nobody's really done before. I do a lot of work before we get to the set. I'm open to changes, but I come very well prepared. There isn't a lot that I haven't thought about or considered. In the sex scene with the fireman, I suggested, "Let me do an orgasm with the sound of a fire engine," or with the priest, "Let me do it like 'Ave Mariaaaaa!' Let me try different things." You don't know if one's going to be too much or not enough, so it's nice for the editors, producers, and director to have a few choices.

There are times when you can't keep a straight face, and there are times when the show is very serious. Whether it's the lesbian female ejaculation or funky spunk or when Samantha cries, "We're all alone, Carrie," the entire team, but the producers and writers especially, have done a fantastic job of treading that fine line between poignancy and honesty and reality and half-hour comedy. I don't even think of us as a half-hour comedy anymore. I think of it as a mini film each week.

THE SWEET SMELL OF SUCCESS When I was literally a starving young actress with no money, eating McDonald's hamburgers for thirty cents for dinner, no one would give me shit. I was waitressing, and I didn't have a green card because I was from Canada. I had no money. I would cut my own hair or cut it really short so I wouldn't have to go to a hairstylist. I had nothing. And now that I'm on this successful TV series, people can't give me enough running shoes or lipsticks.

The first time I was nominated for an Emmy, I was truly overwhelmed. I was crying, because it was the culmination of years of working hard and trying and hoping that I would get jobs and work with people that I respected, and suddenly it's here. And it's here in a way that is so unexpected, especially since it's a show that I had originally turned down.

LOOKING FOR MR. GOODBAR Women who have been "sexually free" or "promiscuous" have been punished through the ages. Whether it's *Looking for Mr. Goodbar* or Mata Hari or Sappho, whatever the scenario has been about a woman being sexual and being up front about her sexuality, each time she was punished, killed, or abused for it—until recently.

The show has made it okay for women to talk about what they like and don't like sexually. It's raised the bar for honesty. I think the show is about the struggle to find intimacy and the struggle for wholeness and completeness.

Samantha-isms

ON WITHHOLDING SEX: "A guy could just as easily dump you if you fuck him on the first date as he can if you wait until the tenth."

ON THREESOMES: "The only way to do a threesome is to be the guest star."

ON POWER AND SEX: "The only place you control a man is in bed. If we perpetually gave men blow jobs, we could run the world."

ON WHY SHE SHOULD TRY HAVING SEX WITH MR. TOO BIG AGAIN: "Because it's there."

ON WHAT DEFINES FRIENDSHIP: "I don't put my dick in you."

ON BAD KISSERS: "If their tongue's just going to lay there, what do you think their dick's going to do?"

ON FUNKY-TASTING SPUNK: "It's so disappointing. Like getting a bad bottle of Beaujolais Nouveau the first day of the season."

ON THE PROSPECT OF NOT GIVING A GUY HEAD AGAIN: "I never even thought of that."

ON *THE RULES*: "The women who wrote that book wrote it because they couldn't get laid. So they constructed this whole bullshit theory to make women who can get laid feel bad."

ON WHY SEX IN AN ILLICIT AFFAIR IS SO GOOD: "They design it that way."

ON WHETHER SHE SWALLOWS: "Only when surprised."

ON PREMARITAL SEX: "Before you buy the car, you take it for a test drive."

ON UNDERSTANDING A MAN: "You can lay your pussy on a table right in front of one and still not know what he's thinking."

ON DATING A WOMAN AND HAVING SEX WITH A STRAP-ON: "With all the fucking and talking, I had no idea men had to work so hard."

ON LEISURE TIME: "My weekends are for meeting new guys so I don't have to keep fucking the old ones."

ON MARRIAGE: "Marriage doesn't guarantee a happy ending. Just an ending."

THE MEN*

The stars of *Sex and the City* are the women, but some of their most emotional moments happen in the company of their five long-term men: Mr. Big, Aidan Shaw, Steve Brady, Trey MacDougal, and Stanford Blatch. The women's problems feel real because the male characters feel real, too—the men are brave and intelligent and they don't let their partners get away with anything.

The first two recurring male characters were

Mr. Big (Chris Noth) and **Stanford Blatch** (Willie Garson), both of whom were featured in the pilot. Mr. Big won our hearts as the mysterious man-about-town Carrie kept running into at parties, and though we didn't know it then, he would later become the first real love of her life. Stanford, with his adorable shrug, was like Carrie's guardian angel, even half jokingly offering his hand in marriage ("Who else will buy you expensive shoes and encourage you to cheat?"). **Steve Brady**

(David Eigenberg), the bartender, with his sweet nature and straightforward menschiness, came in during Season Two as Miranda's much needed ray of sunshine. **Aidan Shaw** (John Corbett), the rugged furniture designer, first appeared in the third season to provide a stable contrast to the elusive Mr. Big. And **Trey MacDougal** (Kyle MacLachlan) appeared shortly thereafter, when he saved Charlotte's life, and stole her heart.

The women on the show are so magnetic and powerful that they would never fall for pushover men. Noth, Eigenberg, Corbett, and MacLachlan are Real Men, with just as much **humor**, brains, and charisma as the gals. "We've always tried our best to keep the guys as palpable and as present as the women," says executive producer Michael Patrick King. "The guys have to be really worthwhile opponents. That's why there are four stars playing them, because our girls are superstars."

*big, strong, smart, funny, cool, grown-up, childish, cocky, careless, clueless, rich, poor, sour, and sweet

MR. BIG

PLAYED BY CHRIS NOTH

If one relationship on *Sex and the City* symbolizes the intoxicating dance of intimacy, it is Carrie and Mr. Big's. From the moment Carrie dropped her purse in front of him on a midtown street, the electricity between them sizzled from off the screen. It didn't matter that he saw her condoms spill onto the sidewalk, or even that he didn't have a first name. Worldly, sophisticated, and driven, he was Carrie's perfect match—although he wasn't necessarily made in heaven. Each time Carrie looked for signs that Big felt strongly about her, he shimmied ever so slightly away.

"Big's been through a marriage," says Noth. "He knows the cost of getting out or in so he's always trying to keep one foot in his own independent world but, at the same time, allow another person to be in his life."

hospital, Carrie stood in front of the automatic hospital doors, looked at Big, exhausted, and said, "We're so over, we need a new word for over." Although we wanted to applaud her for her bravery, we secretly rooted for the two of them to work it out. Because time and time again, Big was there for her when she needed him most—when she felt lonely, was strapped for money, or when everyone else let her down. When Charlotte told Carrie, "I always thought that you two would wind up together," it was hard for anyone to disagree.

Big's tendency to slip back in when we least expected it made him as addictive to us as he was to Carrie. By the end of the fourth season, some fans felt he had returned too many times, while others wanted him to stay for good. According to co-executive producer Cindy Chupack, "In those

The chemistry between Carrie and Big was so strong that no matter how many times they broke up, they always managed to wind up in each other's arms. "Carrie and Big are really good together," says Sarah Jessica Parker, "when they are both, as Michael Patrick calls it, 'up in their stuff.' It's when they both think they're in control."

Carrie and Big dated and broke up twice before reuniting for their illicit affair—which ended when his wife, Natasha, caught Carrie in the apartment and broke her tooth while running down the stairs. After Natasha was taken to the

last episodes of Season Two when he and Carrie were together, right around 'Ex and the City' when he got engaged to Natasha, he became so charming. Chris and Sarah Jessica had such good chemistry that no matter what we wrote or how much of a cad we wanted to make him or how impossible we wanted that relationship to seem, I would go down to the set and think, *How do we pull these two apart?*"

And Big certainly has his share of fans. In the middle of the fourth season, when Big and Carrie's relationship became platonic, a group of Big loyalists showed up at the HBO offices

"The negotiations of intimacy can be difficult for men who have established themselves–
how far they'll go before they feel like they are compromising their own life but still wanting to include someone in it." –CHRIS NOTH

BIO: A graduate of the Yale School of Drama, Noth has appeared extensively in New York and regional theater. Prior to his role as Mr. Big, Noth was best known as Detective Mike Logan on *Law & Order*, a role he played from 1990 to 1995. His film credits include *Double Whammy*, *Cast Away*, the independent films *Searching for Paradise*, *A Texas Funeral*, *Getting to Know You*, and *Naked in New York*. He has been nominated for a Golden Globe for his role as Mr. Big.

"She could reach me,
but I could never get her."
—MR. BIG

in midtown Manhattan with red balloons (the gift Big had given Carrie for her thirty-fifth birthday) and a placard that read, "Don't let Mr. Big fly away."

In the Season Four finale, when Big and Carrie went for a carriage ride in Central Park and shared a kiss, they encapsulated old-time New York and old-time romance. Big called it "corny," and Carrie called it "classic." They might have been describing their own relationship. With their bowling, seedy hotels, cigars and smokes, Sinatra and Mancini, they could be corny but were always classic. Despite his exasperating qualities and his tendency to break our heroine's heart, somehow Big was the only guy that ever seemed a big enough man for Carrie.

A CONVERSATION WITH
Chris Noth

"WHO'S DARREN STAR?" When my agent called and said HBO was doing this new show and Darren Star wanted to meet with me, I said, "Who's Darren Star?" My agent told me he did *Melrose Place*. I thought, *God, I'm not interested in those kinds of shows*. I don't mean to be pejorative, but it wasn't my bag. But when I read the pilot, it was a completely different cup of tea from the other shows. I loved the last scene, where Carrie asks if Big's been in love, and he says, "Absofuckinglutely." I thought that line was a brilliant ending to a show that seemed to be just about sex. So I met with Darren, and he hired me.

SOAVE BOLLA I don't think I'm a sex symbol. Big exists in relation to Carrie. The writers find universals in Carrie and Big and their struggles to commit or not commit. They are able to tap into things that people have been through and relate to. So it's a sexy relationship.

I wasn't a totally happy camper the first six or seven episodes in terms of how Big was being written, but Michael Patrick King and Darren were open to my suggestions. I didn't want Big to be just a symbol in Carrie's life that represented success and elusiveness. I wanted Big to be human. I wanted some disorder within the relationship, and in the phrasing of how he says things or looks at things. I said to the writers, "Flesh it out and don't keep me in this world of 'Soave Bolla' [the cheap wine]. I don't know how to act it." When Carrie punched me, when she farted in bed, I felt like we got into some great human stuff and I could bring more to it. Whenever they write something, I try to take it as far as I can.

LADIES' UNDERWEAR I never felt like "We are men on a women's show." It's great to be amongst all these women, finding out what kind of underwear they are going to wear for a scene. I have learned that you should never interfere with a woman who's getting her hair and makeup done. Sarah Jessica almost took my head off once because I'd been off the show for a while and I was saying "Let's go. What's holding us up?" She said, "Shut up and get in your place."

THE OTHER MEN Carrie had a couple false starts with other men before Aidan, and I was always happy they didn't work out. Everyone wants to feel irreplaceable. Sarah Jessica always made me feel very special, which is why, later on, I got a little jealous and possessive. I thought she was doing the same thing with John Corbett, who I adore. He's one of the most fun guys in the world, but around the end of Season Four, I was feeling the pangs of one foot out the door and one foot still in it. It had gotten to the point where I would walk down the street and everyone would call me "Mr. Big." That was an alarm bell that it was time to move on to the next role. But it was a little bit sad for me.

AIDAN SHAW
PLAYED BY JOHN CORBETT

Aidan Shaw is the embodiment of the good boyfriend, the one every girl wishes she had. Accessible, loyal, and devoted, he is the anti-Big through and through. In creating the character, the writers envisioned Aidan as a new foil for Carrie, a man who would be there for her consistently and force her to examine her own commitmentphobia. "We named the character 'Aidan,'" creator Darren Star recalls, "because initially we wanted to cast Aidan Quinn in the role. We had the idea of a guy who made furniture, who was incredibly down-to-earth, and who was all about heart and not about anything superficial."

Star was already a fan of *Northern Exposure* star John Corbett, and when casting director Jennifer McNamara suggested his name, Star felt he was perfect. "I met with him, Michael Patrick King, and Sarah Jessica," Star remembers, "and John and Sarah Jessica really hit it off."

We first met Aidan when Carrie and Stanford took a trip to his furniture store. She flirted lasciviously and he immediately responded. As they started to date, Aidan revealed himself as a straightforward and winningly old-fashioned guy—he told her he couldn't date a smoker (so she quit), and that he didn't want to jump into bed too quickly (so they didn't).

The more devoted Aidan acted, the more restless Carrie became (in typical New York neurotic style), until she finally started sleeping with Big again. When she confessed the truth to Aidan, he was so pained it was hard not to sympathize. When she asked whether her cheating couldn't just be like a flaw in wood, he replied, "I just know myself. This isn't the kind of thing I can get over," and left her.

As soon as Aidan disappeared, his fans jolted into action. On Corbett's fan site, Aidan lovers were asked to send in miniature wooden chairs and Popsicle sticks urging HBO to bring Aidan back: "Write on the wood itself (if possible), or a separate piece of paper: 'Don't Leave Aidan Unfinished!'" Fans took note, and soon HBO was bombarded with miniature chairs and other pieces of furniture. "We had already made a decision to keep John on," recalls Michael Patrick King, "but it was a really good validation."

A few episodes into Season Four, Aidan did return—thinner, hipper, and more irresistible. The unlikely duo gave it another shot, trying to resolve their differences and develop something long-lasting. "Sarah Jessica and John were genius at finding sweet, very real moments together," says writer and co-executive producer Cindy Chupack, "I think because of their mutual respect, trust, and comfort level." For example, in "Sex and the Country," in which Carrie tried to make herself at home at Aidan's country house, Corbett opted to sing one of his lines to Parker—"Pack your bags, little lady, you're coming to the country with me."

"John likes to sing a lot," says Parker. "If he feels uncomfortable with a line and needs to find a way to make it comfortable for himself, he'll sing it."

Aidan was the first man Carrie lived with and the first who asked her to marry him. He was devoted and crazy about her, calling her "Nuts" and "Lovebird." When she confessed she had had an abortion, he didn't judge her. Carrie couldn't help but love someone who loved her unconditionally, and at times it was impossible not to envy her for having landed such a generous, caring man. Their

"Men and women are different species.
We are never going to understand each other fully." –JOHN CORBETT

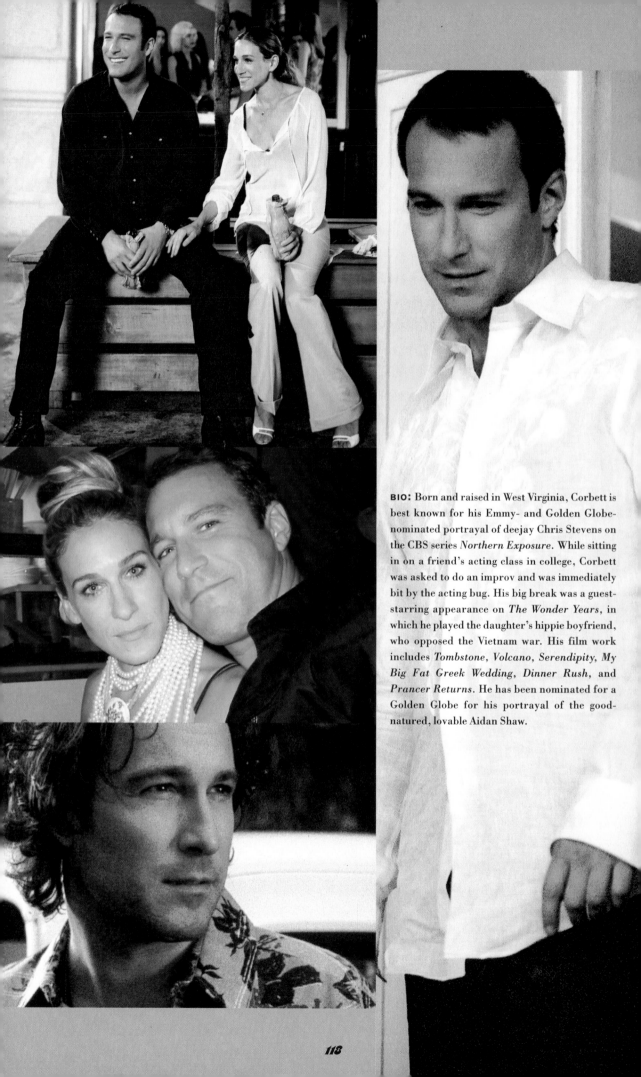

BIO: Born and raised in West Virginia, Corbett is best known for his Emmy- and Golden Globe-nominated portrayal of deejay Chris Stevens on the CBS series *Northern Exposure*. While sitting in on a friend's acting class in college, Corbett was asked to do an improv and was immediately bit by the acting bug. His big break was a guest-starring appearance on *The Wonder Years*, in which he played the daughter's hippie boyfriend, who opposed the Vietnam war. His film work includes *Tombstone*, *Volcano*, *Serendipity*, *My Big Fat Greek Wedding*, *Dinner Rush*, and *Prancer Returns*. He has been nominated for a Golden Globe for his portrayal of the good-natured, lovable Aidan Shaw.

"Is this all because
I suggested getting Maui'd?"
—AIDAN SHAW

biggest fight was over her shoe closet—yet even then, they found a way to compromise.

Despite their closeness Carrie became uncomfortable with her engagement, deciding she needed more time, and a wounded Aidan left her for good. When he packed his bags after helping her fix her toilet, he was thoroughly Aidanesque—kind till the very end.

"When we were breaking the stories at the beginning of Season Four," recalls Chupack, "we had one of those little chairs from a fan on the writers' conference table. When John finally left again at the end of that season we gave him that chair, signed by the writing staff. I think it meant a lot to him that he was so loved by fans outside and inside of the show."

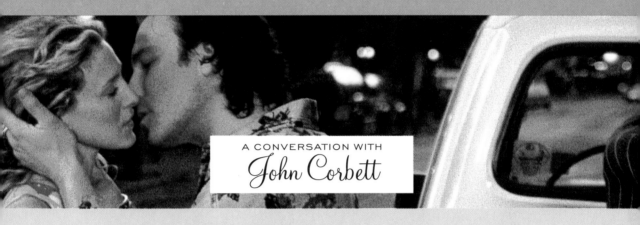

A CONVERSATION WITH
John Corbett

FROM THE COUNTRY TO THE CITY When they offered me the role I wasn't really sure I wanted to do it. I was building a house in West Virginia and I didn't want to stop what I was doing just to work on a show that I had never seen before. I hadn't seen *Sex and the City* because I didn't have cable. I still don't. I think if you do a show for HBO they should give you lifelong cable. When I read Aidan's first few scripts I thought they were very funny. And I thought Sarah Jessica was great—I knew her from films like *L.A. Story* and *Honeymoon in Vegas,* so I was interested in working with her. I made the right choice because there's no one more fun to work with than she is. The first scene we ever did together was on Carrie's stoop, right before Aidan finds out she's a smoker. When the scene begins it's supposed to be as if we are in the middle of a conversation, having fun. As the camera came toward us I said, "Hey, would you like to smoke some crack? I could jet home and get some," and without missing a beat, she responded, "I bet you can jet." We both laughed and the camera found us. From that moment on, I loved working with her.

THE NEW AIDAN When I found out I would be coming back for Season Four, I was so excited. I didn't know about the mail campaign that the fans were doing until after I was back shooting. I have the chair the writers gave me on my shelf. It was so sweet of them to give it to me. I was glad when Michael Patrick King asked me to lose weight because I needed an excuse to lose it. I like to eat, drink, and not exercise. I lost about fifteen pounds and lifted a couple weights. Then I cut my hair and it was enough to show a difference.

WARM APPLE PIE I learn a lot from watching the show, just like the fans do. I'm not there for the coffee-shop scenes so when I see them, it's for the first time. I've learned that women are more promiscuous than I imagined them to be. I've taken them off the pedestal that I had them on, thinking that they were kind of better than me and all my thoughts. The show has some of the finest writers in the business, writing the greatest words for four of the best actors that could ever say those lines. The women are perfectly cast for their characters, and we have seventy talented people filming it and putting it all together. What's not to like? Everybody likes warm apple pie with ice cream. This show is like that. It's universal.

STEVE BRADY

PLAYED BY DAVID EIGENBERG

Bar owner. Aspiring hoops player. Watcher of *Scooby-Doo*. Steve Brady is the quintessential Good Guy. The first word Steve spoke to Miranda the night she walked into his bar was "please"; she was ordering a glass of wine and he immediately called her on her bossiness. Instead of walking out, she stayed, since she was long overdue for meeting someone decent. "There is something about those Steve and Miranda scenes," says Cynthia Nixon, "that allows for silence. There's more acting room, whereas the scenes with the women are so verbal."

Each time Steve and Miranda broke up, this quiet chemistry pulled them back together. After Steve had a testicle removed, Miranda gave him a "mercy fuck" and wound up getting pregnant with his baby. Later on, when she was pregnant and so horny she was about to explode, he gave her a mercy fuck of her own. When the baby was born, Miranda named him Brady, and Steve cried. It was a typical Miranda-Steve moment: if Miranda could be reserved with her emotions, Steve was the sunshine that melted her icy surface.

A STEVE IS BORN

JENNY BICKS: David came in to audition for a bunch of different parts before, and he was so embarrassed by doing sex scenes. In our audition room it's a bunch of women sitting in front of a guy who has to come for them. David just couldn't do it because he is shy, but we knew when he walked in that we wanted him to play something. I had a huge crush on him as soon as he walked in. That's one of the benefits of running a show: you can cast the person you have a crush on. Michael Patrick King and I just turned to each other and said, "That guy, forget about it. He's adorable." So we actually wrote the part of Steve with him in mind. He is fantastic in it.

DAVID EIGENBERG: I heard that the character was written with me in mind. I was flattered, but it made it a little bit harder to read because I wondered, *How do I play myself?* For my other auditions for other roles, all I saw were little scenes of the guys, and I thought the show was only about sex. When I got cast as Steve, I called my mother and sister to let them know. My mother said, "What's the show?" I said, "I don't know if you want to watch it, there's a lot of sex in it." She said, "Well, what am I going to see?" And in my first episode, I had to have an orgasm.

JENNY BICKS: The Steve-Miranda story was very much based on a relationship that I was having at the time. The relationship subsequently ended, but then, ironically, because we wrote so many good things about Steve, I got back together with the guy. People would phone me after the episodes and say, "Steve is so special. I can't believe he would do that for her." I thought, *Oh my God, they're right.* So when we got back together, it was art imitating life imitating art.

CYNTHIA NIXON: When David came on, I was relieved to finally have someone who would stay for a while. I thought, *Well, if I feel this way, Miranda must be thrilled to finally have a guy where she doesn't have to explain who she is for two hours and then find out if she likes to kiss him.* I like working with David so much, and Steve is such a good foil for Miranda. Miranda is so defensive and ready to reject before she is rejected that it was nice to see her with someone who was steady and calm and knew that he was in love with her. Steve was a man she couldn't indict. It made her think, *What is there in me that is afraid to get close to somebody?*

"I don't know exactly what happened with Steve's intelligence. I suppose it might reflect on me, but the first episode of the show Steve was reading Hemingway, and he has gone from that to watching *Scooby-Doo*. But he's very observant. He finds value in life." —DAVID EIGENBERG

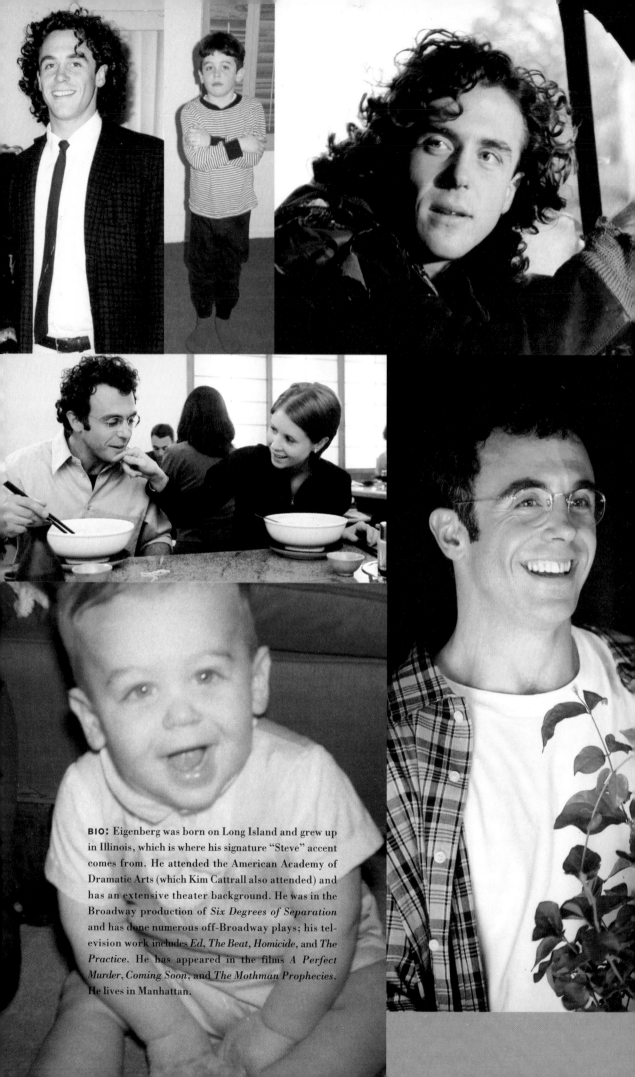

BIO: Eigenberg was born on Long Island and grew up in Illinois, which is where his signature "Steve" accent comes from. He attended the American Academy of Dramatic Arts (which Kim Cattrall also attended) and has an extensive theater background. He was in the Broadway production of *Six Degrees of Separation* and has done numerous off-Broadway plays; his television work includes *Ed, The Beat, Homicide,* and *The Practice.* He has appeared in the films *A Perfect Murder, Coming Soon,* and *The Mothman Prophecies.* He lives in Manhattan.

"Jesus, Miranda.
It's like you're the guy sometimes."
—STEVE BRADY

A CONVERSATION WITH

David Eigenberg

BEING A MAN ON THE SHOW My life on the show has always been about enjoying the moment, because as a guy on the show, you never know when you're going to get the axe. You have to enjoy it for what it is. I've said goodbye a couple of times and then gotten calls to come back.

Cynthia Nixon is an amazing actress and a great person to be around. I think we work in a similar way and we can goof around together. The cancer stuff was pretty heavy, but between takes we were grab-assing and laughing. Early on, Michael Patrick King had asked me, "What do you think happens to Steve and Miranda?" I said, "I don't know if they can be together or not. I know they're a great couple, but I don't know if they can make it. I think Steve should get cancer and die, except it should never be morbid and he should laugh through the whole thing." And Michael said, "That's not going to happen."

STRONG WOMEN People come up to me and say, "Hey, Steve, I love the show, character is wonderful, I love you guys together." Some people say, "She's not good enough for you," or "Stay with her." People tell me they're sorry about my loss. And somebody told me in all seriousness, "Whether you have a boy or a girl, all I wish is that you have a healthy and happy baby."

The show has ruined my dating life, though. Most single women between twenty-five and forty know the show, so whenever they say hi to me, I immediately go into Steve mode. I become less cynical and sarcastic than I am in life. I know the women are connecting to something that's not necessarily me. As a result, I tend to seek out women who don't know about the show.

I'm like Steve in that I've always been attracted to strong women. I like a woman who has her own sense of herself, is not quick to defer to a man, and stands on her own two feet. I also like conflict in a relationship, because there's nothing better than when you have a good fight and then you have sex.

When I'm not working on the show, I do construction. It's not that I love it, I actually kind of loathe it, but I need structure in my life. Wracking my knuckles across the boards is good for me.

This show has been one of the highlights of my life. In light of September 11, when people are wondering whether to stay in New York, I can say, "You know what? It's scary living in New York these days, but I've lived a good life and I'm not leaving, and *Sex and the City* is part of the reason it's a good life."

TREY MACDOUGAL

PLAYED BY KYLE MACLACHLAN

Charlotte predicted her own marriage at the beginning of Season Three when she announced on the Staten Island Ferry that this was the year she would get married. In due time, Dr. Trey MacDougal careened into her life. If Charlotte is the quintessential dreamer, Trey was her perfect match. When he admitted that he married her "because I thought it was time. I'm of a certain age. People expect you to get married," Charlotte responded, "That sounds familiar."

What defined their marriage was the never-ending succession of obstacles to their fantasy of wedded bliss. Charlotte inadvertently proposed, and Trey responded, "Alrighty." Together they dealt with impotency, Charlotte's infertility, their different views on having children, and Trey's overprotective mother, Bunny (who went bed shopping with the new couple, watched Trey take a bath, and inadvertently walked in on Trey and Charlotte having sex). Trey was everything Charlotte wanted, except for the umbilical cord tied tightly around his neck.

With his deadpan delivery, Kyle MacLachlan made Trey lovable even at his most excruciating moments—like when Charlotte walked in on him masturbating to *Juggs* magazine. When they finally decided to separate at the end of Season Four, he dutifully returned to the apartment to pose for a *House & Garden* photo. Throughout all the conflicts we yearned for their marriage to work. Because, let's face it, what woman doesn't want to be married to Kyle MacLachlan?

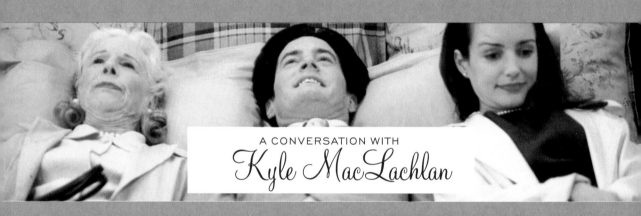

A CONVERSATION WITH
Kyle MacLachlan

PLAYING A CHARACTER WITH IMPOTENCE When I found out I would be playing an impotent character, I wasn't exactly thinking, *Yeah! That's a great idea! That's the kind of dilemma I'd like to tackle.* But I knew the focus in the plotline was going to be on how Charlotte would react to this problem. So much of her character, and ultimately mine, too, was about the collision between what she was hoping marriage would be and what it was.

THE MRS. MACDOUGALS Kristin Davis is such an easygoing person and a lot of fun. But she also really knows her character and is very specific in her acting. She has a great sense of comedy but can also play a little pain behind the eyes. She gets that beautifully. I also loved working with Frances Sternhagen, the actress who plays Bunny. What I love about her most are her sense of humor and her sense of lightness. She is really good at what she does and doesn't have to prove anything.

THE BATTLE OF THE SEXES Men tend to glaze over the surface a little bit, skip across the water. Men are there, and then bang, they're on to the next thing. Women can get men to take a step back and do a little more self-examination. That was part of the dynamic between Charlotte and Trey. She got him to slow down and think about other things. Men don't communicate like that. We're better at talking about the components than the wiring.

BIO: MacLachlan made his feature-film debut in David Lynch's *Dune* and also starred in Lynch's *Blue Velvet*. He first became known to television audiences with his Emmy-nominated role as FBI agent Dale Cooper in Lynch's *Twin Peaks*. His feature work includes Michael Almereyda's *Hamlet*, *Timecode*, *The Trigger Effect*, *Showgirls*, *Miranda*, and *Me Without You*. He made his directorial debut in 1993 with an episode of HBO's *Tales from the Crypt*.

"One of the strongest things about the show is that there is a friendship that exists between these women. Regardless of what happens to them, what they say to each other, they will still be there for each other." —KYLE MACLACHLAN

STANFORD BLATCH

PLAYED BY WILLIE GARSON

If Carrie were asked to make a list of her very best friends, she would most certainly include the three girls, but somewhere on it would also be sweet Stanford Blatch. A gay talent manager with a penchant for monochrome suits and pithy bon mots, Stanford and his dating sagas make Carrie's seem like a trip to the beach. He wins our hearts with his mischievous sense of humor, shiny bald pate, and perseverance in the face of the often bizarre and brutal gay dating world.

His crushes have included his underwear-model client, who turned out not to be gay, and a blind date who took one look at him and said, "I'm sorry, it's not going to happen." Later came his online lover, BigTool4U, whom he arranged to meet at a club where he was forced to check his pants at the door, and Anthony, Charlotte's wedding planner, who wrote him off as "Ed-I-Have-No-Hair-is."

When Carrie made a new gay friend, an Australian shoe distributor named Oliver, Stanford suddenly had to compete for Carrie's (platonic) company. He called her greedy and Carrie later admitted, "I'd been so preoccupied with my gay boyfriend, I kept forgetting about my gay husband," realizing that her bond with Stanford could be just as possessive as any romantic one. Tipsy Stanny trumpeted his long history with Carrie and then kissed Oliver on the lips, a moment that was thoroughly Stanfordesque. We knew that Carrie might make new friends, and even new gay ones, but Stanford Blatch himself was irreplaceable.

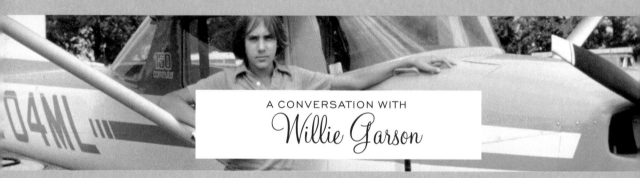

A CONVERSATION WITH
Willie Garson

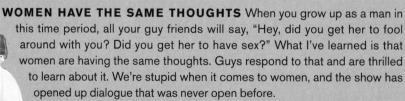

WILLIE AND SARAH Sarah Jessica Parker and I have been friends for almost twenty years. We were set up a long time ago. Someone thought we'd really get along, so we were seated next to each other at a dinner party, and we became absolutely great friends. When Sarah told me she was doing the show, I said, "You're kidding. I'm going to do it, too." She said, "Oh my God, you have to do it." We always say if either of us was on the show and the other one wasn't, we'd be there anyway, hanging out.

There are little aspects of Sarah's and my relationship that we try to get in the show. Carrie's always reaching over and patting Stanford's bald head, which is something Sarah Jessica does in our life. Sometimes, right before we roll, she'll ask me to say something to make her laugh, because I can make her laugh in a second. I can quote any line from *The Jeffersons,* and Sarah will be in peals of laughter and then we can start the scene.

WOMEN HAVE THE SAME THOUGHTS When you grow up as a man in this time period, all your guy friends will say, "Hey, did you get her to fool around with you? Did you get her to have sex?" What I've learned is that women are having the same thoughts. Guys respond to that and are thrilled to learn about it. We're stupid when it comes to women, and the show has opened up dialogue that was never open before.

BIO: Garson was trained at the Actor's Institute in New York and is a graduate of Wesleyan University. He has made more than two hundred appearances on such television shows as *Friends*, *The X Files*, *The Practice*, and *NYPD Blue*, and has had recurring roles on *Party of Five* and *Melrose Place*. His film work includes *There's Something About Mary*, *Groundhog Day*, *Kingpin*, and *Being John Malkovich*. Garson continues to work in theater with Naked Angels, Manhattan Theatre Club, and the Roundabout Theatre Company.

"I've learned from doing the show that women want and enjoy sex as much or more than I do as a man."
—WILLIE GARSON

Carrie

	KURT HARRINGTON (LOATHE OF HER LIFE)	DEREK (UNDERWEAR MODEL)	MARRYING GUY	JARED THE NOVELIST	NEW YANKEE	MAN WITH NO SOUL	MAN WITH TWO FACES	MAN WHO STEALS CHEAP USED BOOKS FOR NO REASON	SINGLE, STRAIGHT SMOKER	JEREMIAH THE CATERER
DIDN'T										
DID										
	SAM THE TWENTY-SOMETHING (TIMOTHY OLYPHANT)	GUY WHO LEFT MONEY (FRENCH ARCHITECT)	MR. BIG	BEN (THE NON-FREAK)	SETH (JON BON JOVI)	FUCK BUDDY	THE ALCOHOLIC (DENIAL GUY)	BILL KELLEY ("TO PEE OR NOT TO PEE")	THE BI GUY	AIDAN SHAW

Miranda

	THE MODELIZER	SYD THE LESBIAN	THE COUPLE (THREESOME VALIDATION)	SAMANTHA'S ACCOUNT-ANT	CONSTRUC-TION WORKER	FRIEND WHO MARRIES DECORATOR	MARRIED GUY (COMEDY CLUB)	HAIR-PLUGS GUY	GUY IN WINDOW (TURNS OUT TO BE GAY)	SANDWICH
DIDN'T										
DID										
	SKIPPER	SPANK-VIDEO GUY	CATHOLIC GUY	DIRTY TALKER ("YOU LOVE A FINGER IN YOUR ASS")	GUY SHE FAKES IT WITH (OPHTHAL-MOLOGIST)	GUY WHO WATCHES PORN	STEVE BRADY	PUBLIC-PLACES GUY	ANGRY GUY	DIVORCED DAD

Samantha

	SIDDARTHA (TANTRIC CELIBACY GUY)	DEN-OF-INIQUITY GUY ("SLAP ME HARD")	GUY FROM WEDDING (SAW SOMETHING HE LIKED MORE)	PAKISTANI BUSBOY	DICK CRANWELL (HIS WIFE TRIES TO RUIN HER)	SEVENTY-TWO-YEAR-OLD	COUPLE NEXT DOOR	TWO GAY GUYS (THWARTED THREESOME)	KEVIN THE MASSEUR (WON'T GO DOWN)	GUY AT RESTAURANT
DIDN'T										
DID										
	CAPOTE DUNCAN	BARKLEY THE MODELIZER (LIKES TO VIDEOTAPE)	CHARLOTTE'S DOORMAN	JON THE TWENTY-SOME-THING	HER REALTOR	MARRIED GUY	THE TURTLE (BERNIE TURTLETAUB)	YOGA-CLASS GUY	JAMES (SMALL-DICK GUY)	THE "WE" GUY

Charlotte

	CAPOTE DUNCAN	MARRYING GUY (WRONG CHINA)	TRADER AT BEAR STEARNS	PROZAC GUY	CROTCH ADJUSTER	CHEATING GUY (KISSES SOMEONE ELSE)	POWER LESBIANS	BUSTER (SHOE SALESMAN)	DOUBLE-BOOKED GUYS	GETS-IN-FIGHTS GUY
DIDN'T										
DID										
	UP-THE-BUTT GUY	SHMUEL (HASIDIC FOLK ARTIST)	BLOW-JOB GUY (GUY WITH DOG)	THREESOME GUY	THE RABBIT	MR. PUSSY	MR. FIX-IT	THE WIDOWER	GUY AT WEDDING	UNCIR-CUMCISED GUY

128

SHORT STORY WRITER (PREMATURE EJACULATOR)

DR. BRADLEY MEEGO (GOOD ON PAPER)

DAWN (ALANIS MORRISETTE)

PHOTOGRAPHER

WADE (COMICS GUY)

THE DATING GAME

In their first four years on the air,
the girls on *Sex and the City*
have dated, tried to date, and refused to date
quite a few Manhattan men.

RAY KING (JAZZ GUY)

As Miranda put it, "Who would have thought an island so small could hold all of our boyfriends?" Some dates lasted only till the first kiss, while one turned into marriage. One of the gals tended to bed everyone she met, while another went all the way only when she was sure it was something special (hint: it wasn't Charlotte). Take a walk down the girls' hall of fame and see who they "did," and who they "didn't."

PHONE-SEX GUY

LEW (WON'T SWALLOW FOOD)

CAFETERIA GUY (BRACES DATE)

DEAD GUY

ASSHOLE

CAPTAIN CRUNCH (THINKS SHE'S STUCK UP)

SPEED-DATING GUY (FAKE ER DOCTOR)

CHLAMYDIA GUY

THE DETECTIVE

OPEN-DOOR GUY

MARATHON MAN (TUCHUS LINGUS)

INTER-PRETER (SEX WHEN PREGNANT)

SEX-SWING GUY (MALE SAMANTHA)

NYU WRESTLING COACH (THE LOST ORGASM)

BED-ON-WHEELS GUY

DILDO MODEL (GARTH)

CALEB MACDOUGAL (HOT SCOT)

FRIAR FUCK

THREESOME GIRL

RICHARD WRIGHT (BROKE HER HEART)

CHARLOTTE'S BROTHER

MARIA (SONIA BRAGA)

BABY TALKER (MBA)

GUY WHO WANTS HER TO SHAVE

J.J. (GOSSIP COLUMNIST)

THE OTHER SAM JONES

OVER-THE-HILL LOSER

GUY NOT BOTHERED BY TRANNIE NOISE

THE LIGHTNING BOLT (THOR THE TRAINER)

DÉJA FUCK

GUY WITH SERVANT

DOMINIC (THE EX)

SPORTS GUY

HERSELF

MR. TOO BIG

RICKY THE FIREMAN

SHORT GUY

HER ASSISTANT

CHIVON (SISTER HATES HER)

YOUNG MCDONALD

WEEKEND GUY

GUY WITH FIANCÉE (POLITICAL PARTY)

GUY WITH EX (USED-DATE PARTY)

SLOPPY KISSER

MARRIED FRIEND

GUY AT PLAYBOY MANSION (WANTS TO BUY HER SOME BOOBS)

TREY'S GARDENER

DIVORCED GUY (FROM MOMA)

LATE-NIGHT GUEST (LET THIEF IN)

VIAGRA GUY

MOVIE STAR

GAY-STRAIGHT MAN (PASTRY CHEF)

FELL-ASLEEP GUY

TWENTY-SOME-THING (GAVE HER CRABS)

DRAG-KING GUY (DONOVAN LEITCH)

"YOU FUCKING BITCH, YOU FUCKING WHORE!"

TREY MACDOUGAL

ADAM BALL (FUNKY SPUNK)

The fourth season of *Sex and the City* broke all the rules.

Carrie agreed to marry Aidan, then, against television convention, broke off the engagement—and he left her. Miranda slept with Steve to show him he was sexy, one ball or two, and became pregnant with his child. Samantha, who had dated practically every man in Manhattan, became involved with a woman—and later fell hard for a man who betrayed her. Charlotte discovered she couldn't conceive, and her differences with Trey grew so irreconcilable they decided to separate.

Engagement, divorce, pregnancy, abortion, cancer, fertility, death of a parent—in its fourth season the series dealt with potent, meaningful issues. Yet it managed to do so in its own way, with irreverence and a lack of preciousness.

As the characters became richer, the actresses were given ample opportunity to demonstrate their range. Kristin Davis showed Charlotte's heartbreak at the realization that Trey and she wanted very different things out of their marriage. Kim Cattrall revealed Samantha's humanity when she fell in love with Richard Wright. Cynthia Nixon made us weep in the episode when her mother died. And Sarah Jessica Parker, who had already made Carrie the ultimate sympathetic everygirl, displayed uproarious comedic chops in the fashion show episode and touching vulnerability when Aidan left her, and again when Big left New York.

The final episode, "I Heart NY," written by Michael Patrick King, was a tearjerker to top all tearjerkers. As an autumn leaf fell from a tree and Carrie picked it up, musing, "Perhaps if we never veered off-course, we wouldn't fall in love or have babies or be who we are. After all, seasons change. So do cities. People come in your life and people go," we could only wonder how she would be able to dust herself off and start all over again. And yet we knew we couldn't bear for her not to, and felt ever more optimistic that after all her struggles, she would someday meet her equal, a man with the same charisma, love of life, and humanity she possessed. In the meantime, we knew she'd have her friends. And despite so many highs that it was hard to imagine how the show could get any better, we couldn't wait for the ladies to come back in full force.

THE FOURTH SEASON *

*the fashion show fright, the ring that's not right, the two boys who fight, and Samantha's Mr. Wright

1

THE AGONY AND THE 'EX'-TACY

WRITTEN AND DIRECTED BY *michael patrick king*

"Soul mates– reality or torture device?"

Charlotte confronts Trey about their sex life and is confronted by a bit of his sex life–on her leg; Samantha finds religion when she meets a fabulous friar; Carrie gets stood up by her friends at her thirty-fifth birthday party, but one of them manages to surprise her by showing up at her house with red balloons.

CINDY CHUPACK (CO-EXECUTIVE PRODUCER):

My parents and my sister (who's married with three kids) came to see the Season Four premiere with me. I had just turned thirty-five and was without a boyfriend and feeling a little alone, and as we were watching this episode that Michael Patrick King wrote and directed so brilliantly, I remember thinking how true it was, and how complicated the feelings are about getting older and feeling alone. I thought, *Now I don't have to explain any of this to my parents. I can just say, "Yep, that's how I feel. That's what it's like."* I felt so proud of our show in that moment. It's validating to be part of a show that tells it like it is.

2

THE REAL ME

WRITTEN AND DIRECTED BY *michael patrick king*

"No matter how hard we look, do we ever see ourselves clearly?"

Carrie gets in touch with her inner supermodel when she's asked to be in a fashion show; Samantha gets in touch with her inner nude model when she has revealing photos taken; Miranda indulges her sexual confidence when a man at the gym finds her sexy; Charlotte learns that her vagina is depressed.

MICHAEL PATRICK KING (EXECUTIVE PRODUCER):

I saw the jeweled panties we used in this episode at a fashion show and thought how great Sarah Jessica would look in them. Then I said to her, "I have this image of an electric—" and she said, "—blue trench coat?" And I said, "Yeah. Electric-blue trench coat." She said, "I was just thinking of that." I said, "I wonder if anybody is making it." Two days later, Dolce & Gabbana showed an electric-blue trench coat in their new line, and we got it.

NICKI LEDERMANN (KEY MAKEUP ARTIST):

We had all these young models on set for this episode, and every straight male on set was drooling over them. The girls were so cool. Heidi Klum was a sweetheart. Sarah Jessica bruised her hand pretty badly during the falling sequence, but she was a trooper. She did it herself for every take.

CARRIE: *When I first moved to New York and I was totally broke, sometimes I would buy Vogue instead of dinner. I just felt it fed me more.*

132

3

DEFINING MOMENTS

WRITTEN BY *jenny bicks*
DIRECTED BY *allen coulter*

"What really defines a relationship?"

Carrie's new "friend," Mr. Big, interferes with her dating life when she meets a jazz musician named Ray King; Trey's sex drive improves, but only to the point where he can do it when he might get caught; Miranda dates a guy so comfortable in the relationship that he leaves the bathroom door open—for number two; Samantha becomes a lesbian.

MICHAEL PATRICK KING:

You never see Carrie open the door to her building—until this episode. The people who live there like the show and decided to let her go in. It's when she goes out with Big, and he wiggles his eyebrows at her, and she says, "Nightie-night." She opens the door and goes inside. We said, "Yes! She went in! Four years and she finally got in her door!"

4

WHAT'S SEX GOT TO DO WITH IT?

WRITTEN BY *nicole avril*
DIRECTED BY *allen coulter*

"What comes first, the chicken or the sex?"

Carrie has mind-blowing sex with Ray King, but isn't sure what she feels for him; Samantha experiences the joys of an emotional relationship; Charlotte eventually agrees to move back in with Trey; Miranda goes on a sex strike (although she's the only one affected)—then becomes addicted to chocolate as a substitute.

KIM CATTRALL (SAMANTHA)**:**

The lesbian plotline was not just about the sexual thrill but about intimacy, for Samantha. I had the fortunate experience of working with Sonia Braga, who is this incredibly sexy Brazilian gorgeous woman. If there is anything that was weird about it, it was that both of us are so innately heterosexual. But if I ever had any questions about being a lesbian, they were squelched in those episodes, because I felt absolutely nothing. Or maybe she's just not my type.

CINDY CHUPACK:

There was talk in the writers' room about how much we needed to see when Maria ejaculates. Michael felt adamantly that you needed to see it, and he and Jenny demonstrated it with a bottle of water. Jenny had the bottle between her legs, Michael pretended to be about to go down on her, Jenny squirted him, and we all died laughing. You had to admit, you needed to see it.

CARRIE: *How does that work? You go to bed one night, you wake up the next morning, and poof, you're a lesbian?*
MIRANDA: *I forgot to tell you: I'm a fire hydrant.*

133

5

GHOST TOWN

WRITTEN BY *allan heinberg*
DIRECTED BY *michael spiller*

"When a relationship dies, do we ever really give up the ghost, or are we forever haunted by the spirits of relationships past?"

Miranda is worried that she has a ghost in her apartment; Carrie and Miranda attend a party for Steve's bar—which Aidan has designed— and Carrie has a run-in with the ghost of her relationship past; Bunny walks in on Charlotte and Trey in bed; Maria wants to talk about Samantha's past relationships, and Samantha, sick of the emotional chow-chow, breaks up with her.

MICHAEL PATRICK KING:

When we decided to bring Aidan back in the fourth season, I went to John Corbett and said, "Johnny, we want to bring you back differently to show that we are not just a television show bringing a character back. We want to bring you back as a guy who has a changed attitude, and the only criticism we have ever heard is about your hair and your weight," even though I loved his weight. John said, "I knew I was a fatty." And I said, "John, the season where you had a little bit of extra weight on showed people that you could act. And now we can bring you back rock-hard and give Carrie lines about the new and improved Aidan." He said, "I get it."

6

BABY, TALK IS CHEAP

WRITTEN BY *cindy chupack*
DIRECTED BY *michael spiller*

"In matters of love, do actions really speak louder than words?"

Miranda meets a guy in her running group who puts his tongue where no man has gone before; Charlotte and Trey talk about having a child; Samantha puts on fake nipples and attracts an M.B.A. who turns out to be a B.A.B.Y.; after Carrie tells Aidan she misses him, he agrees to give the relationship another shot.

CINDY CHUPACK:

We had had "Lick-the-Butt Guy" written on the writers' board forever, and none of us, especially the women, really wanted to write that one. Finally I was working on this episode, and the theme was "Actions speak louder than words," and it wound up in there. I felt like I wrote it in a way that made it palatable—if I can use that word in this context—because Miranda said in the coffee-shop scene, "Is this what we're doing now?" There were enough different points of view in that scene to reflect all of our varied points of view. When the episode aired, my dad said something like "I hope you don't experience everything you write about!"

CARRIE: *How did they get the message that the ass is now on the menu?* MIRANDA: *I bet there's one loudmouthed guy who found some woman who loved it and told everybody, "Women love this."* CARRIE: *Who is this guy?* MIRANDA: *Who's the woman who loved it?* SAMANTHA: *Don't knock it until you try it.*

134

CARRIE: *Aidan, you can't keep punishing me, and I can't keep punishing me. I made a mistake and I am sorry, and I know that you can't forget what happened, but I hope that you can forgive me. You have to forgive me. You have to forgive me. You have to forgive me. You have to forgive me, Aidan. You have to forgive me. You have to forgive me.*

TIME AND PUNISHMENT

WRITTEN BY *jessica bendinger*
DIRECTED BY *michael engler*

"Can you ever really forgive if you can't forget?"

Charlotte quits her gallery job to have a baby; Miranda has a neck spasm, and Carrie sends Aidan to help; Samantha starts an affair with a guy who won't forgive her for having hair; Carrie feels Aidan is punishing her for her affair with Mr. Big.

CYNTHIA NIXON:

Sometimes you can use nudity as a laugh, like the scene where Aidan picks me up off the bathroom floor when I have a neck spasm. They wanted to be able to see a little bit of my body so that it would look more embarrassing and it wouldn't look like I was all covered up. It was funny.

MY MOTHERBOARD, MY SELF

WRITTEN BY *julie rottenberg & elisa zuritsky*
DIRECTED BY *michael engler*

"Why were so many independent women . . ."

Then Carrie's computer crashes, and Aidan is overly supportive; Miranda's mother has a heart attack and dies suddenly; Charlotte micromanages the girls' trip to the funeral; troubled by Miranda's mother's death, Samantha has difficulty with her orgasms.

MICHAEL PATRICK KING:

When Miranda's mother died, we got into a huge discussion about Miranda's economic background. Everyone in the writing room had a different feeling. I come from a lower-middle-class/working-class Irish Catholic family, and I imagined Miranda's mother to be my mother and Miranda to be the smartest, the one who got out. We decided to make Miranda from a specific Mainline Philly family, but we didn't acknowledge the father.

CHARLOTTE: *Sex can still be great without an orgasm.* SAMANTHA: *That is such a crock of shit.* CARRIE: *She has a point.*

135

9

SEX AND THE COUNTRY

WRITTEN BY *allan heinberg*
DIRECTED BY *michael spiller*

"In a relationship, when does the art of compromise become compromising?"

Steve learns he has testicular cancer, and Miranda supports him through surgery; Carrie the city girl struggles to make herself at home in Aidan's country house; Samantha visits for the weekend and meets a hay-chewing stud and his cow; Charlotte walks in on Trey taking a bath while his mother is in the bathroom.

KYLE MACLACHLAN (TREY):

For that scene when Charlotte finds Trey taking a bath with Bunny in the room, I kept going further and further. I started out just being in the tub and turning around and smiling and pretty soon I felt like Marilyn Monroe or something. I was washing my leg, my leg was up in the air, and then I was scrubbing under my arms. It became less a scene about Charlotte's reaction and more about me scrubbing my body.

10

BELLES OF THE BALLS

WRITTEN BY *michael patrick king*
DIRECTED BY *michael spiller*

"Are men just women with balls?"

Steve feels less manly now that he has only one ball, so Miranda offers some assistance; Mr. Big, lovelorn over a girl, visits Carrie at Aidan's country house and the two men get into a fight; Trey is offended when Charlotte asks him to get his sperm tested; Samantha tries to get a job doing PR for hotel magnate Richard Wright and cries when he says he'd hire her if she were a man.

CHRIS NOTH (MR. BIG):

Michael Patrick King and I spent a whole dinner talking about the story line between Big and Willow Summers, because something a little similar had happened to me at some point in my life. I had said to a friend of mine, "She could reach me, but I could never get her," and I told Michael that. He took that and created this incredibly great scene.

MICHAEL PATRICK KING:

When I told John Corbett he and Big were going to have a fight, he said, "But I'm going to win, right? Because it's like the Green Hornet and Batman." That's where the Green Hornet came from. The interesting thing about the fight scene was that both those guys wanted to win. I told Chris, "You can't win. You have won for three seasons. You cannot win today." It was a Greek tragedy. Aidan is light, Big is dark. Light must win in that moment. But I told them there could never be a punch thrown, because as soon as someone hits, it is not a comedy anymore.

CARRIE: *Balls are to men what purses are to women. It's just a little bag, but we feel naked in public without it.*

11

COULDA, WOULDA, SHOULDA

WRITTEN BY *jenny bicks*
DIRECTED BY *david frankel*

"Are we there yet?"

Miranda is pregnant with Steve's baby and can't decide what to do; Charlotte discovers she may never get pregnant; Carrie and Samantha reveal that they have had abortions; Samantha is hired, then fired, by Lucy Liu after she tries to use her celebrity connections to snag a Birkin bag.

JENNY BICKS (CO-EXECUTIVE PRODUCER):

This was the hardest episode I've ever written. It was just so tough to balance the weightiness of the issue that you are writing about, with the humor that you want to inject in it, with the truth of the times, which is that women have had abortions. I think if you take a group of four women, at least one of them will have had one. So it was time we talked about it on the show.

SARAH JESSICA PARKER (CARRIE):

I worked a lot with Michael Patrick and Jenny on this script. The issue is so complicated, and I felt the characters had to have a lot of different feelings about it, even if they are pro-choice. The issue of Carrie having had an abortion wasn't as important to me as how she felt about it and how she articulated it to Aidan, to Samantha, and to the other women. Miranda's decision had to be the center of the episode, but I didn't want it to mean nothing for Carrie.

12

JUST SAY YES

WRITTEN BY *cindy chupack*
DIRECTED BY *david frankel*

"In matters of love, how do you know when it's right?"

Samantha and Richard, her new boss, join the mile-high club in his private jet; Miranda tells Steve she's pregnant with his child; Charlotte starts taking fertility drugs only to find that Trey isn't sure he wants a baby; Carrie says yes when Aidan asks her to marry him.

SARAH JESSICA PARKER:

We shot the engagement scene on the street Woody Allen and Soon-Yi Previn live on, and later we saw them up in the window watching us. I thought it was so interesting that one of the great filmmakers of certainly *my* lifetime was interested in watching anybody else shoot anything. David Frankel, who has been very influenced by Woody Allen, was directing the episode. The movie I made with David Frankel, *Miami Rhapsody*, is a real homage to the type of movie that Woody Allen does. David was talking to me, and I was pointing toward the window to show him they were watching, but we all had to gesticulate so it didn't look like I was pointing. It was pretty neato.

AIDAN: *I love you, Carrie. There's no one I could love more. I want to live my life with you.*
CARRIE (VOICEOVER): *Maybe there are no right moments, right guys, right answers. Maybe you just have to say what's in your heart.* **CARRIE:** *Yes.*

137

13

THE GOOD FIGHT

WRITTEN BY *michael patrick king*
DIRECTED BY *charles mcdougall*

"What are we fighting for?"
Carrie and Aidan, cramped in their joint apartment, struggle with space issues; Richard and Samantha dance by his pool; Miranda is one horny mama; Trey buys Charlotte a cardboard baby to make her feel better (it doesn't work).

KIM CATTRALL:

In the rooftop scene, you see Samantha trying to take control, and then someone has more control than she does, and you see her deal with that. It's a great opportunity as an actress, because I get to explore being human instead of just mining the comedy gold. Everybody's expecting "bada-boom," and what you get is so unexpected from Samantha. No matter how much Samantha doesn't want to get hurt, the challenges and the hoops the writers make her go through are what I love about her. She's brave and tenacious but also incredibly vulnerable.

14

ALL THAT GLITTERS...

WRITTEN BY *cindy chupack*
DIRECTED BY *charles mcdougall*

"To be in a couple, do you have to put your single self on a shelf?"
Carrie, the going-out gal, bristles at Aidan's desire to stay at home; Samantha tells Richard she loves him and immediately regrets it; Charlotte and Trey's differences cause them to separate; when Miranda's coworker outs her as pregnant, she accidentally outs him as gay.

CINDY CHUPACK:

When we were filming the scene where Aidan wanted to stay in and Carrie wanted to go out, John Corbett was so charming and sweet that there was no way you understood why she was leaving him, even though she was just saying the words I wrote. I laughed about it, went up to Michael's office, and said, "I don't know why she's leaving him. We are going to hate her because he seems like this great guy." Michael said, "No, go back down there and have them do it again." I went back down and asked the director if John could just be a little bit more of an asshole, in his own world, not so attentive to her and so cute. John made a few adjustments and it made a big difference.

CARRIE: *He fell asleep, and I watched gay porn.* **SAMANTHA:** *That's what happens when people say, "I love you."*

15

CHANGE OF A DRESS

WRITTEN BY *julie rottenberg & elisa zuritsky*
DIRECTED BY *alan taylor*

"Do we really want these things, or are we just programmed to think we do?"

Carrie wonders whether she's the marrying type; Samantha contemplates monogamy; Charlotte enrolls in a dance class and decides to kick up her heels; Miranda fears that her maternal instinct may never kick in.

SARAH JESSICA PARKER:

When we were shooting the breakup scene at Columbus Circle, this man came around in a big garbage truck. He was covered with tattoos, and he came around a couple of times, wanting to say hi to me, which was very, very sweet. I came over and met him, and he asked me to pose for a picture with him, and he wound up putting an ad in the *Village Voice* thanking me and saying if I ever wanted to get together to give him a call.

16

RING A DING DING

WRITTEN BY *amy b. harris*
DIRECTED BY *alan taylor*

"What's it all worth?"

Carrie's money troubles make her doubt her self-worth; Samantha receives expensive presents from Richard but wants the one gift he won't give; Charlotte can't decide what to do with her engagement ring; Miranda and Steve grapple with the challenge of raising a baby together but not *together*.

SARAH JESSICA PARKER:

Carrie has no gal Friday. She is her own gal Friday. She doesn't make a lot of money, and she makes bad choices with her money, but she has never been anything other than completely independent. I worked a lot on the speech to Charlotte. I said, "What? Charlotte's going to tell Carrie about being responsible when Carrie has taken care of herself her whole life?" Carrie works because she has to, even though she happens to like her job. She lives in a not beautiful, rent-controlled apartment, thank God. Charlotte got to judge Carrie about having an affair, and Carrie never judges Charlotte. Carrie has stood by her and supported her. So I said, "Carrie has every right to say, 'You are my friend. How could you not offer me the money? I wouldn't have taken the money, but you should have offered it.'" I wanted people to know that Carrie could be a financial mess, but the fact of the matter is she has nobody to turn to but herself.

CHARLOTTE: *Carrie, I love you. But it is not my job to fix your finances. You are a thirty-five-year-old woman. You have to learn how to stand on your own.*
CARRIE: *Charlotte, what is that on your finger?*

17

A VOGUE IDEA

WRITTEN BY *allan heinberg*
DIRECTED BY *martha coolidge*

"How much does a father-figure figure?"

After meeting a paternal editor at *Vogue,* Carrie tries to figure out whether her problems with men have to do with her own father; Samantha fulfills Richard's birthday wish to bring a little more love into their relationship; Charlotte hosts Miranda's baby shower; Miranda wonders whether she has the mother gene.

MICHAEL PATRICK KING:

The photograph of Carrie as a little girl in this episode is actually Sarah Jessica at three in a field. No one else was in the actual photograph, but we put in a father, John MacDonald, one of our cameramen, though we were skittish about getting into Carrie's family history. But we found a way to cut it together when Carrie asks Miranda whether her problems with men are because of her father leaving, and Miranda says her father came home every night at seven, and Carrie says it's a crap shoot. So we get out of blaming Carrie's love life on her family, but we did take a step.

BEHIND-THE-SCENES TIDBIT:

For the scene where Miranda puts the baby down at the baby shower and ignores it and he slides off the couch, Kim Cattrall suggested the trick that was used in the show: putting the baby on a baby blanket that was underneath the frame so that the blanket pulled the baby.

18

I HEART NY

WRITTEN BY *michael patrick king*
DIRECTED BY *martha coolidge*

"Can you make a mistake and miss your fate?"

When Carrie learns that Mr. Big is leaving town, she is nostalgic about their relationship and New York itself; Samantha is convinced Richard is cheating on her; Charlotte isn't sure she's ready to get back in the singles scene; Miranda meets her new significant other.

CYNTHIA NIXON (MIRANDA):

Michael Patrick talked to me about my pregnancy and labor stories when he was working on this episode. During my labor I had my boyfriend there, but I also had a girlfriend with me. She was a very calming influence, similar to how Carrie is for Miranda, and before the delivery it was pretty quiet and focused. When we shot the scene, it was really exciting because the babies were so great. We had about fifteen different babies on set.

SARAH JESSICA PARKER:

The narration at the end of "I Heart NY," which was written before September 11, is just so prophetic and shocking. It talks about how cities change and people come and go and catastrophic events happen and you move on. It's fall and it's cold again, which we've never done. So Michael Patrick has instincts that are really slightly remarkable.

CHARLOTTE: *Miranda has a son!* SAMANTHA: *Just what the world needs. Another man.*

We Heart New York

"The city to me was always the fifth character on the show," says creator Darren Star. "People don't visit the same restaurant every day. They go out, so the city is their living room." One of the great pleasures of watching the show, for New Yorkers and non-New Yorkers alike, is the joy of seeing the city come to life. It's hard to imagine Carrie, Charlotte, Miranda, and Samantha living anywhere else in the world, so central is New York to their fashion sensibility, endless stream of adventures, and uniquely Manhattanesque blend of romanticism and cynicism.

"These women wouldn't be the same in Milwaukee, Boston, Chicago, or Cincinnati," says Sarah Jessica Parker. "If Carrie lived in a small town that was a crossroads, she wouldn't walk out a door and not know what the future holds. **In New York City, you walk out the door and you do not know what is going to happen. There's such potential for poetry."** The writers base many of their stories on events that happen to them in the city—everything from the roosters on Carrie's roof to the loud transsexuals outside of Samantha's apartment to Miranda's having the Chinese-food place on speed dial. "The city is a great turbine engine for everything you write," says executive producer Michael Patrick King. "It's a conveyor belt for characters and bachelors and people coming

and going. You have the city, the four girls, and some broken hearts. Go."

Co-executive producer John Melfi, production designer Jeremy Conway, and the location department (led by Seth Burch in the first four seasons) work each week to do just that—find locations where the girls can have their hearts broken and, once in a while, mended. They look for bars, clubs, and restaurants that feel authentically New York and of-the-moment. "These women are in the know," says Burch, "so we shoot in hot spots to give the show a sense of style."

While New York has a great history of filmmaking, many crews tend to shoot a touristy version of the city that focuses only on well-known landmarks. "On *Sex and the City*," says Melfi, "we try to have a location make sense for the scenes. We'll go to a historic location like the Old Town Bar, where Carrie went on a date with the Yankee, and we'll be careful not to damage the mirrors or the booths because it's a staple of New York and we want people to know that that's a real bar. We're really proud to be able to shoot in these places."

When the show uses interiors, it relies on the generosity of bar and restaurant owners for the use of their locations. Because it pays a relatively small amount for the use of spaces, the people who offer them do so for many reasons. For businesses, the exposure can help bring in customers, while for individuals, it can be exciting to see their homes on TV. In seeking out locations, the crew looks for appropriateness, shootability, and cost effectiveness,

DARREN STAR: New York was always glamorous to me. I remember coming to New York as a kid, going to the theater and restaurants and, in the days of Studio 54, thinking that New York was the place to be. I created *Central Park West* as an excuse to get myself to New York. When I met Candace Bushnell, she took me to Bowery Bar when it was at its peak. Carolyn Bessette was at our table, David Blaine was doing card tricks, and it was a down-the-rabbit-hole kind of feeling. I thought, *These people are a million times more interesting than any of the people I'm writing about on Central Park West*. That's when I began to think that I wasn't capturing the real New York in the show I was doing, and that I wanted to create a show that did.

JENNY BICKS: We hear people talking about the show all the time in New York. It is such a validation in New York to feel like people are so into the show that it becomes their life. Once I was in Moomba and the people at the next table were incessantly talking about Carrie's affair. And I thought, *God, I guess we did something right*.

but their first priority is to bring the scripts to life in the best way. When the writing focused on more internalized, long-term relationship stories in Season Four, the scenes took place less often in the city and more often in the women's apartments. HBO made a specific request to the producers to get more of the city in, recalls Melfi. "The studio said, 'What happened to New York?' so we had to go back and start figuring out how we could open up the show, add some walk-and-talks, and get some more environment in. Sometimes you are servicing the characters, and then you forget about your unwritten fifth character, your city. It's a balancing act."

Whenever possible, the producers strive to shoot within the five boroughs of New York City, even when the plotline takes place somewhere else. The Hamptons episode in Season One, when Carrie visits her married friends, was shot in a Manhattan brownstone; the Season Two Hamptons episode was shot in Queens and Staten Island; and though the actual Staten Island Ferry was used, the fireman's bar was in the West Village.

The mayor's office provides permits for all film and television crews shooting in the city and bends over backward to be accommodating—unlike other cities, New York does not charge for police officers or permits that let the show shoot in the street. The New York City Police Department's movie and television unit provides the officers needed to close streets off to moving traffic and pedestrians. "These guys know filmmaking," says Burch, "and they love coming to our set because we don't do stunts, we don't do gunshots, and we have good-looking women."

The cast and crew are prouder than ever to have the privilege of shooting in the city after the September 11 terrorist attacks on the World Trade Center. The Season Four finale, "I Heart NY," which was written by Michael Patrick King and filmed before September 11 but aired several months later, was as much a love letter to New York as a farewell to Mr. Big. Carrie and Big's carriage ride through Central Park was a return to a city of innocence, and the choice of "Moon River" on the sound track was an affectionate nod to the classic New York film, *Breakfast at Tiffany's*. The episode was dedicated to "our City of New York . . . then, now, and forever." As Carrie's final voiceover told us, "It's comforting to know the ones you love are always in your heart," it was hard not to weep at the emotional bruise the city had suffered.

"There is so much humanity in New York," says Parker. "People were surprised about the compassion that New Yorkers revealed on September 11 because, for the most part, New Yorkers cling to a solitary existence. But people wouldn't live here if they did not love other people. It is impossible to live here and not be a people person."

MICHAEL PATRICK KING: One time I went out to dinner with Chris Noth and Sarah Jessica. Chris has a vintage Mercedes from 1970. We pulled out of a parking garage and came to a red light, so we stopped. I was in the back seat, Chris was driving, and Sarah Jessica was next to him. A couple pulls up in a car next to us, and they look over, and the guy says, "Ooh, it's real. I knew it."

There are seven wonders of the location-scouting world—places so challenging to shoot in they are virtual Mount Everests of filmmaking: a high-rise, an airport, a stadium, a major hotel, a boat, Times Square, and a highway. By the end of Season Four, the show had shot in five of them—the USTA National Tennis Center in Queens (which doubled for Yankee Stadium); the Plaza Hotel (where Carrie reads a poem at a wedding); the Staten Island Ferry (the firefighter episode); the top of a high rise (Richard Wright's pool); and the streets of Times Square (when Carrie dates the comic-book artist). Other locations such as the Monkey Bar and the Central Park Boathouse have also served as eye-popping locations.

the map

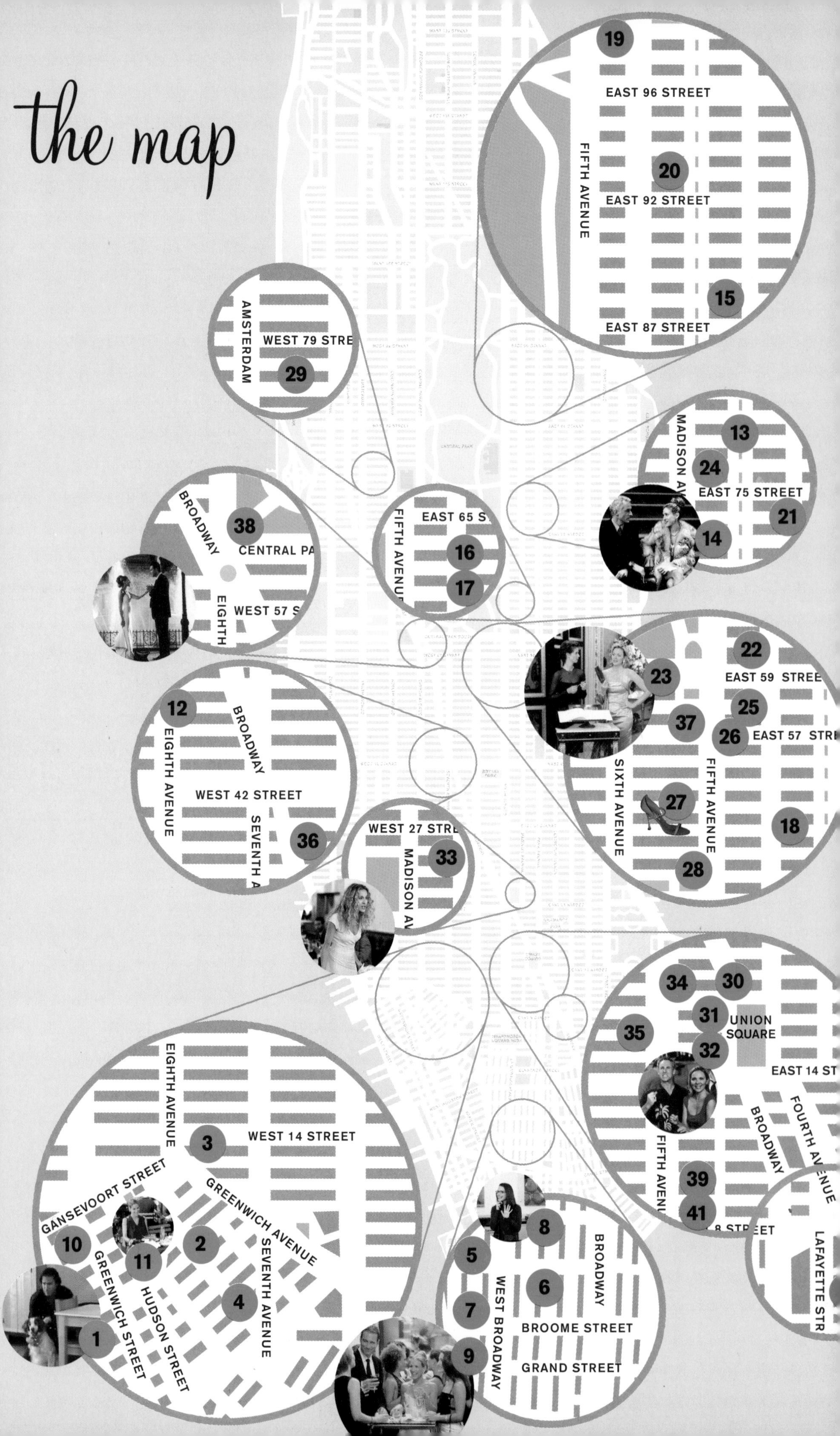

19
EAST 96 STREET
20
EAST 92 STREET
15
EAST 87 STREET
FIFTH AVENUE

AMSTERDAM
WEST 79 STRE
29

BROADWAY
38
CENTRAL PA
EIGHTH
WEST 57 S

FIFTH AVENUE
EAST 65 S
16
17

MADISON A
13
24
EAST 75 STREET
14
21

22
EAST 59 STREE
23
25
37
26 EAST 57 STR
27
18
28
SIXTH AVENUE
FIFTH AVENUE

12
BROADWAY
EIGHTH AVENUE
WEST 42 STREET
SEVENTH A
36

WEST 27 STRE
33
MADISON AV

34 **30**
31 UNION SQUARE
35
32
EAST 14 ST

EIGHTH AVENUE
WEST 14 STREET
3
GANSEVOORT STREET
GREENWICH AVENUE
10
2
11
4
GREENWICH STREET
HUDSON STREET
SEVENTH AVENUE
1

FIFTH AVEN
39
41
8 STREET
BROADWAY
FOURTH AVENUE
LAFAYETTE STR

8
5
6
7
WEST BROADWAY
BROADWAY
BROOME STREET
GRAND STREET
9

In its first four years on the air, *Sex and the City* has shot at hundreds of real bars, restaurants, and stores—all plotted out for you on the *Sex and the City* map. Use it as a guide for your own walking tour of Manhattan, or just reminisce about your favorite moments as you discover where the girls have wined, dined, dated, and debated.

WEST VILLAGE

1. Furniture Company
Aidan's furniture store

2. Magnolia Bakery
Miranda and Carrie eat cupcakes

3. Nell's
The girls play drag-queen bingo and run into Samantha's transvestite ex

4. Pleasure Chest
Miranda, Carrie, and Charlotte buy vibrators

SOHO

5. D&G
Carrie takes the New Yankee to the Dolce & Gabbana party, and Charlotte brings her "low-hanger" boyfriend

6. Helena Rubenstein Beauty Gallery
The girls take a sauna here, and, surrounded by naked women, Charlotte feels self-conscious about her body

7. Hotel Venus
Carrie and Charlotte go lingerie shopping

8. Louis K. Meisel Gallery
Charlotte's gallery

9. SoHo Grand
Richard Wright's black-and-white ball

MEATPACKING DISTRICT & CHELSEA

10. Samantha's Apartment
300 Gansevoort Street
This is Samantha's official address although it doesn't actually exist

11. Pastis
Carrie and Oliver have brunch

12. Collins
Miranda first meets Steve

UPPER EAST SIDE

13. Charlotte's Apartment
700 Park Avenue
This is Charlotte's official address although it doesn't actually exist

14. Carrie's Apartment
245 East 73rd Street
Five different locations have been used to denote the exterior of Carrie's building, but this is her official address, which does not actually exist

15. Church of the Holy Trinity
Charlotte and Trey get married

16. Hermès Boutique
Samantha orders the Birkin Bag with the help of Lucy Liu's name

17. Madison Avenue and 63rd Street
Big picks Carrie up in his car and tells her she's not the marrying kind

18. Monkey Bar
Carrie and Big, dressed to the nines, have drinks

19. Mount Sinai Hospital
Miranda has a baby

20. 93rd Street between Park and Madison
Aidan proposes to Carrie

21. Payard Patisserie & Bistro
Miranda buys chocolate cake and goes on a sex strike

22. Barneys New York
The Upper East Side mecca of the latest and the finest in designer trends

23. Plaza Hotel
Carrie shows up outside the Plaza after Big's engagement party to Natasha
Terrace Room: *The bouquet falls to the ground at Miranda's decorator's wedding*

24. Vera Wang Bridal House
Charlotte buys her wedding dress

25. Tao
Carrie and Ray King run into Big and his model girlfriend

26. Tiffany & Co.
Trey buys Charlotte's engagement ring

27. Manolo Blahnik
The gold standard, the crème de la crème. Sex and the City put these high-end, sexy shoes in the popular lexicon.

28. Jimmy Choo
Carrie's other favorite shoe store

UPPER WEST SIDE

29. Miranda's Apartment
331 West 78th Street
This is Miranda's official address although it doesn't exist

UNION SQUARE

30. ABC Carpet & Home
Charlotte and Trey go bed shopping with Bunny

31. Blue Water Grill
Charlotte and "Gets-in-Fights Guy" have brunch

32. Coffee Shop
Samantha meets the sports addict

33. Eleven Madison Park
Big tells Carrie he is engaged to Natasha

34. Old Town Bar
Carrie dates the New Yankee

35. Paul Smith, Inc.
Miranda and Steve go suit shopping

MIDTOWN

36. Northeast Corner of 41st Street and Broadway
Charlotte meets Trey

37. Brasserie 8 1/2
Lynn Cameron (Margaret Cho) asks Carrie to be in the fashion show

38. Columbus Circle Fountain
Carrie and Aidan break up

EAST VILLAGE & LOWER EAST SIDE

39. Il Cantinori
Carrie's lonely 35th Birthday party

40. Joe's Pub
Big and Carrie meet Ray King

41. Patricia Field Shop
Drag-queen style meets Hello Kitty at this downtown boutique

the Ripple effect

From its restaurants to its bars, its sunglasses to its heels, *Sex and the City* has evolved from a hit TV show into an international trendsetter with an influence more powerful than any fashion magazine or nightlife guide. While TV audiences have always mimicked the clothing and hairstyles of their favorite stars (could anyone forget the "Rachel"?), *Sex and the City* is unique in that it is a virtual how-to manual for New York style and leisure. Because so many of the show's bars and restaurants are real, New Yorkers can dash right over to the same hot-spots frequented by the girls as soon as an episode's over—provided, that is, that they can get a table! Many of these clubs and eat-eries, such as Il Cantinori, Bungalow 8, and Tao, have seen huge surges in their clientele after making their *Sex and the City* debuts. Designers and magazine editors often use the show's war-drobe statements as inspiration for their own clothing lines or fashion spreads. Sometimes the series highlights a fash-ion piece that is already becoming the next big thing (such as Burberry coats); other times the item doesn't catch on until viewers spot it on the stars (fabric flow-ers). But whether it's the chicken or the egg, *Sex and the City* is always on the cutting edge of cool.

RAY-BAN AVIATOR SUNGLASSES: Emotionally bruised from her breakup with Big, Carrie wore these classic Ray-Ban aviators to Yankee Stadium—they then popped up on the peepers of fabulous women all over the country.

NAMEPLATE NECKLACE: Nameplate necklaces had been popular among young African-American and Latina women for many years, and Patricia Field had sold them in her own Eighth Street store long before Carrie began wearing one. "It's nothing unusual, but it wasn't in the white world, so we put it on Sarah Jessica," says Field. "The necklace is a very universal item, which makes it easy to wear."

HORSESHOE NECKLACE: Field discovered the horseshoe necklace, by young up-and-coming jew-elry designers Mia & Lizzie, and knew immediately that Sarah Jessica Parker would like them. Carrie has worn many models of Mia & Lizzie jewelry, including clovers, a heart, and ankle bracelets.

FABRIC FLOWER: Though the fabric flower had been featured on the show as early as the second season, the trend exploded only after Carrie began wearing them when she dated politician Bill Kelley at the top of Season Three. From then on, flowers were blooming everywhere. "Accessory companies were making them," says Field, "and designers were designing dresses with the flower already affixed."

SHORT SHORTS: Remember the shorts trend of the summer of '99? Carrie wore a pair to play Twister with Seth (Jon Bon Jovi) and within weeks, short shorts came back for good.

MANOLO BLAHNIK BOUTIQUE: Parker and *Sex and the City* have done for Manolo Blahnik shoes what Brooke Shields did for Calvins. Though upscale Manhattan women like Candace Bushnell were already devotees of the sexy, fetishizing "limousine shoes" when the show went on the air, the sales have skyrocketed since Carrie began wearing them, despite the fact that learning to walk in them is an art all its own.

THE SJP: In honor of Sarah Jessica Parker, Manolo Blahnik designed a shoe bearing her name—the SJP. An ankle-strap stiletto, it comes in leather, suede, and crepe de chine, and in a variety of colors. It is available at his Manhattan boutique. For fans who have wondered what it's like to walk in Carrie's shoes, now that dream can be a reality!

RUBBER NIPPLES: The fake nipples Miranda and Samantha wear in the fourth season are available at Patricia Field in Greenwich Village. They were designed by Lori Barghini, who, on a party weekend in Las Vegas with her girlfriends, took the shampoo caps off the bottles and stuck them in her bra. She and her friends got such a strong reaction from men that she decided to market them. Barghini met actress Kristin Davis at the Michael Kors fashion show and gave her the nipples. Michael Patrick King thought they would work for the show and it wasn't long before they popped up in the episode.

PLAID FAD: Scot is hot these days, and not only on *Sex and the City*. "I felt that when we broke Charlotte and Trey up we needed a big deal," recalls Michael Patrick King. "Then I read in the *New York Times* that there was a New York Scottish Society annual fling, and I thought, *Let's fling her at the fling.* I said to Patricia Field, "I want to have Charlotte totally in plaid," and then all of a sudden *Town & Country* came out with a spread on a really high-end Tartan party, which was all done in Burberry. That happened with the kilts, too. Kyle MacLachlan is Scottish and I was looking for some interesting comic choice for Trey. I thought about him wearing a kilt at his wedding, and he said, "I have a kilt." I said, "Let's get them married in a kilt," and then boom—Guy Ritchie is wearing a kilt when he marries Madonna."

BIRKIN BAG: The Birkin bag costs about as much as a small car but that doesn't stop women in the know (like Samantha) from craving one on their arm. Designed by Hermès in honor of actress Jane Birkin, who complained in the sixties that she couldn't find a bag large enough to hold everything she wanted, the current waiting list for the bag is actually years long, although celebrities do get special preference.

HORSEHEAD BAG: The horsehead shoulder bag was made by Beverly Hills designer Timmy Woods. Although a bag in the shape of a horse is not exactly an understated fashion statement, Woods saw her orders skyrocket the moment the horse debuted. "That surprised me," says Field, "because it's a big horse's head. It's a little off the edge."

trivia quiz:

1. Who hits on Mr. Big first?

A CARRIE

B CHARLOTTE

C MIRANDA

D SAMANTHA

1.

2. What is Stanford's nickname for his client, Derek the supermodel?

A THE BOD

B THE ROCK

C THE BONE

D THE JETER

3. When Carrie goes to visit Patience and Peter in the Hamptons, what does Peter surprise her with?

A GOOD MUFFINS

B A HOT CUP OF COFFEE

C HIS PENIS

D A MORNING MASSAGE

4. What is the name of the blow-job guy's dog?

A BUTTERSCOTCH

B GOLDENROD

C FLUGELHORN

D HOOVER

2.

4.

5. What gift does Samantha bring to Laney's baby shower?

A BREAST PUMP

B DIAPHRAGM

C BOTTLE OF SCOTCH

D BABY LEASH

6. What is the name of the hit off-Broadway play that Catholic Guy, Miranda's showering stud, writes after they break up?

A *SHOWER OF SHAME*

B *SHOWER POWER*

C *APRIL SHOWERS BRING MAY FLOWERS*

D *WHY DO YOU GLOWER WHEN I SHOWER?*

7. Where does Charlotte hide her Rabbit?

A UNDER THE BED

B INSIDE A BAG OF POTPOURRI

C BEHIND A STUFFED RABBIT

D IN HER UNDERWEAR DRAWER

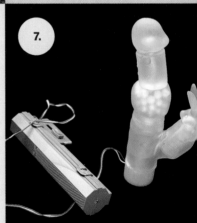

7.

Where did Miranda meet the guy who likes to talk dirty in bed?

- VIETNAMESE LUNCH TRUCK
- HER APARTMENT-BUILDING LOBBY
- COURT
- RUNNING IN THE PARK

8.

9. What is the name of the book written by Samantha and James's couples therapist?

A *WHAT'S LOVE GOT TO DO WITH IT?*

B *MARRIAGE: A USER'S GUIDE*

C *MAPPING THE TERRAIN OF THE HEART*

D *IN-TO-ME-SEE*

. Why do Charlotte and the circumcised guy break up?

- HE'S CONVERTING TO JUDAISM AND DOESN'T WANT TO DATE AN EPISCOPALIAN
- THE PAIN IS SO UNBEARABLE FOR HIM THAT SEX IS IMPOSSIBLE
- HE THINKS SHE WASN'T SUPPORTIVE ENOUGH OF HIS DECISION
- HE FEELS HE NEEDS TO DATE OTHER WOMEN

11. What is inside Ben's freak box?

A *JUGGS* MAGAZINE

B A HUMAN HEAD

C HIS CUB SCOUT BADGE COLLECTION

D A PINUP OF JOHN STAMOS

11.

12. What does Samantha do to psych herself into having sex with Mr. Cocky?

A SMOKES HAWAIIAN GOLD

B TAKES TWO ADVANCED YOGA CLASSES

C DOES RHYTHMIC BREATHING

D ALL OF THE ABOVE

13.

. What is the message on the birthday card Big sends Carrie with the flowers?

- "I ABSOFUCKINGLUTELY LOVE YOU."
- "BEST WISHES ON YOUR BIRTHDAY."
- "HERE'S LOOKING AT YOU, KID."
- "A ROSE IS A ROSE IS A ROSE."

14.

14. What is the name of Charlotte's childhood horse?

A TADDY

B SAMANTHA

C MR. PEEPERS

D BROWNIE

15. According to the *New York Times* Styles section, what song played when Natasha walked down the aisle at her wedding?

A "WHEN A MAN LOVES A WOMAN"

B "LADY IN RED"

C "MOON RIVER"

D "I STILL HAVEN'T FOUND WHAT I'M LOOKING FOR"

16.

16. What lie does Carrie tell Aidan when she first meets him in his furniture store?

A SHE IS A DESIGNER

B SHE IS A NONSMOKER

C SHE IS STANFORD'S GIRLFRIEND

D SHE IS VISITING THE STORE FOR A COLUMN SHE'S WRITING

17. Who gave Miranda chlamydia?

A STEVE, HER BOYFRIEND

B SKIPPER, HER EX

C DAVID, THE ANGRY GUY

D THE MODELIZER

18. What stops Carrie from saying Mr. Big's name when she introduces him to Aidan at the New Designer's Showcase?

A THEY FALL INTO A KIDDIE POOL

B SHE SPILLS COFFEE ON HIM

C NATASHA STUMBLES AND BREAKS HER TOOTH

D SHE GETS ACCOSTED BY ANTHONY, CHARLOTTE'S WEDDING STYLIST

19.

19. What does the funky-spunk guy do for a living?

A RUNS A LARGE CORPORATION

B PLAYS PRO BASKETBALL

C MAKES DOCUMENTARY SHORTS

D CUTS THE COMING ATTRACTIONS FOR FILM COMPANIES

18.

20. Miranda's speed-dating guy lies and says he is a doctor. What is his actual profession?

A USHER AT MADISON SQUARE GARDEN

B ASSISTANT MANAGER OF AN ATHLETE'S FOOT

C CORNER HOT-DOG VENDOR

D STANDING INSIDE A SANDWICH IN FRONT OF BLIMPIE'S

21.

21. What is the name of Carrie's Learning Annex class?

A SINGLE SLAVES OF NEW YORK

B BRIGHT LIGHTS, DATE CITY

C GIRLS, INTERRUPTED

D MANHATTAN MARRIAGE MYSTERIES

2. Which television personality [d]oes Miranda fall in love with [w]hen she goes on a sex strike, [a]nd what does she eat when she [w]atches him?

- JON STEWART; CHOCOLATE ÉCLAIRS
- DAVID LETTERMAN; KNISHES
- CHARLIE ROSE; MICROWAVE POPCORN
- DENNIS MILLER; HOT DOGS

25.

[2]. Who does Steve name his [ca]r after?

- HIS SON
- HIS DOG
- SCOOBY-DOO
- MIRANDA

24. What is Carrie's secret single behavior?

- A SHE BAKES COOKIES AND EATS THEM IN THE BATHTUB
- B SHE SINGS BAD 1980S ROCK BAL- LADS WHILE PAINTING HER TOENAILS
- C SHE KEEPS REORGANIZING HER SHOE CLOSET AGAIN AND AGAIN
- D SHE EATS A STACK OF SALTINES WITH GRAPE JELLY WHILE STANDING UP IN THE KITCHEN READING FASHION MAGAZINES

25. What job does Charlotte get after Trey leaves?

- A DOCENT AT THE MUSEUM OF MODERN ART
- B HER ART GALLERY JOB BACK
- C VOLUNTEER AT MOUNT SINAI HOSPITAL
- D FREELANCE BABY-SHOWER COORDINATOR

[2]6. What does Alexa, the twenty- [o]ne-year-old, call Richard during [th]e threesome with Samantha [th]at makes him so angry?

- SWEETIE
- MY MAN
- DICK
- DADDY

26.

27. What magazine do Trey and Charlotte pose for in their apartment?

- A TOWN & COUNTRY
- B HOUSE & GARDEN
- C WALLPAPER
- D ELLE DÉCOR

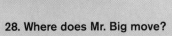

28. Where does Mr. Big move?

- A SILICON VALLEY
- B SUN VALLEY
- C NAPA VALLEY
- D ST. BARTH'S

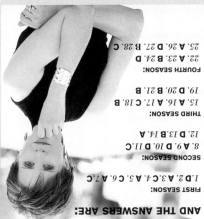

155

GLOSSARY

ABSOFUCKINGLUTELY (adv.): an expression that denotes certainty in a way deliverable only by Mr. Big

ALPHA DOG (n.): the one in a relationship who doesn't want to share the water dish

B

BABY BLUE (n., slang): Viagra

BED ARREST (n.): the state of inertia invoked when your boyfriend makes you cuddle with him all day, thus preventing you from doing your errands and going to spinning class

"BEST" (adj.): the slap-in-the-face salutation at the end of a card given with a gift

BLOW JOB TUG-OF-WAR (n.): the elaborate dance that ensues when a man tries to encourage the woman to go south when she would rather stay far north

BOGART (v.): to keep a guy all to yourself, especially one such as Mr. Pussy

BOX OF FREAKDOM (n.): the home of illicit photos, love letters, old marriage licenses; every guy has one—or does he?

BRAT MITZVAH BEAST (n.): a girl with an upcoming Bat Mitzvah who is relentlessly demanding about her party accommodations

BREAKUP RULES (n. pl.): 1) it takes half the total time you went out with someone to get over them; 2) lie; 3) until emotionally stabilized, enter no stores; 4) never stop thinking about him, even for a moment, because that's the moment he'll appear; 5) no matter who broke your heart or how long it takes to heal, you'll never get through it without your friends

C

CHEATING CURVE (n.): the theory that someone's definition of cheating is in direct proportion to how much she herself wants to cheat

CLAM MOUTH (abstract n., unpleasant): when a guy's tongue just lays there in your mouth like a clam

CLASSIC SIX (n.): 1) an apartment with six rooms—two bedrooms, a living room, a dining room, a kitchen, and a maid's room; frequently found on the Upper West Side of Manhattan; 2) an apartment a guy buys only if he's thinking about marriage

CLICK AND TELL (v.): to take photos of models and reveal which one's a bitch and which one's a bigger bitch

CLIT TEASE (n.): a straight girl who hangs out with lesbians without telling them that she's straight

CODEPENDENT COMING (n.): when a woman fakes orgasms because he's a nice guy and means well

CODE PHRASE (n., common among longtime female friends): the secret phrase that enables people to bow out of a situation early, i.e., "I have to go feed my cat."

D

DÉJÀ-FUCK (abstract n.): the strange sensation that you're fucking someone you've already fucked

DINING-OUT-ALONE ARMOR (n.): 1) a book; 2) a project; 3) the things you bring with you to make being alone in a restaurant less embarrassing

DOUBLE-BOOK (v.): to schedule two dates in one night

DOUBLE-DIP (v.): to date both men and women

DRINK THING (n.): not a drink date but the crucial step before it (origin: vague but definitely male)

E

"EVERYTHING BUT" GIRL (proper n.): a girl who does everything but have intercourse with a guy

F

FAKE A SONOGRAM (v.): to pretend to be excited about the impending birth of a baby boy

FASHION ROAD KILL (n.): a model who falls down on the runway during a show

FAUX CALL (n.): the humiliating but common process of calling an ex and hanging up because you have no idea what you'd say if he picked up

FLIRTINI (n., fabulous): vodka, pineapple, and champagne

"FLO IS COMING TO TOWN" (slang): in Charlottespeak, "I'm getting my period" (see also "See you next Tuesday")

FRENEMIES (n. pl.): two friends who are always fighting it out for everything

FUCK BUDDY (n.): 1) a guy you've had a couple of dates with that didn't really go anywhere, but the sex was so great you keep him on call; 2) not a slave but has a life, a life you don't really have to know about; 3) guaranteed delivery within Manhattan in six hours or less

FUCKINSTEIN (proper n.): a woman who gets harassed by her conservative apartment-building neighbors for having too many late-night guests

FUNKY SPUNK (n.): bad-tasting joy juice

G

GAY-STRAIGHT MAN (n., plentiful in New York City): a new strain of hetero sexual males spawned in Manhattan as a result of overexposure to fashion, exotic cuisine, musical theater, and antique furniture (see also "straight-gay man")

GHERKIN (n., sad): a small penis

GOING-OUT-OF-BUSINESS SEX (n., definitely not abstract): sex you have with someone who's leaving town for good

GOLDICOCKS (proper n.): a woman who can't find a guy with the right size penis

GOOD ON PAPER (adj.): a guy with great credentials whom you always wind up leaving for some hot guy who rides a motorcycle and doesn't have a checking account

GOODY DRAWER (n.): the nightstand drawer in which a person keeps all the sex essentials

GRAND GESTURE (n.): the powerful declaration of a guy's love that makes you reconsider your decision to break up with him

GUEST STAR (n.): 1) the pinch hitter; 2) the girl the couple asks to come in, screw, and leave

I

ILLEGAL DUMPING (n.): when someone dumps you before getting to know you

INTELLECTUAL BEARD (n.): a nonmodel substitute date for a modelizer

ISLAND OF LOST MEN (n., somewhere near I-don't-nesia): the place where men who ask for your number but never call eventually wind up

L

LA DOULEUR EXQUISE (n., French, but familiar to many Americans): the exquisite pain of loving someone unattainable

LANDING STRIP (n.): what some Brazilian bikini waxers leave you when they're done

LAZY OVARY (n., feminine): when an ovary stops producing eggs

LOATHE OF YOUR LIFE (n.): your original, most hated love; e.g., Kurt Harrington

LOW-HANGERS (n. pl.): balls that hang so low they get in the way

M

MADONNA-WHORE COMPLEX (n.): when a man sees a woman as his virginal wife, not his sexual plaything

MANHATTAN GUY (proper n.): a genetically mutant strain of single man that feeds on Zabar's and midnight shows at the Angelika

MARRYING GUY (proper n.): that elusive and rare Manhattan man whose sights are set on marriage

MARTHA STEWART OF DEATH (proper n.): a woman who overcoordinates grief plans

MID-THIRTIES POWER FLIP (n.): the period when an eligible man in his thirties starts to feel that he's holding the chips when it comes to women

MISS DIAL-A-FUCK (proper n.): a woman who calls a man on the spur of the moment, expecting him to come over and have sex with her; in Skipperspeak, Miranda Hobbes

MODELIZER (n., common, esp. in New York City): a man who is obsessed not with women but with models

MONOGAMY (n.): an extremely contagious disease

N

NAKED DRESS (n.): the dress you wear the night you plan to have sex with someone; can be found on the body of Carrie Bradshaw on numerous New York City buses

P

PERINEUM (n.): Latin for "not without an engagement ring"

POWER LESBIANS (n. pl.): Manhattan's latest group to flaunt their disposable income; seem to have everything: great shoes, killer eyewear, and the secret to invisible makeup

R

REAL ESTATE BRIDE (proper n.): a woman who marries to get an apartment

REPRODUCTIVELY CHALLENGED (adj.): in Charlottespeak, barren

S

SAPPHIC SLUMP (n.): a down point in a lesbian relationship

SECRET-SEX GIRL/GUY (n.): the girl/guy you have sex with on the side but are afraid to introduce to anyone you know

SECRET SINGLE BEHAVIOR (abstract n.): the stuff you do when you're totally alone; things you wouldn't want a boyfriend to see you do

SEE (C) YOU (U) NEXT TUESDAY (slang): Charlotte's term for the place where Flo stays when she comes to town (see also "Flo is coming to town")

SEX HAZE (n.): when the sex is really great and you start acting like a crazy person, then start to imagine the relationship is something it's not; especially common in women who have dated Mr. Pussy

SEX LIKE A MAN (n., common in Manhattan): sex without feeling

SEX-ON-A-FIRST-DATE CURSE (n.): the (alleged) curse that if you sleep with someone on a first date, you will never hear from him again

SHARPEI (n.): an uncircumcised penis

SINGLE WOMAN'S SPORTS PAGES (n. pl.): the *New York Times* wedding section

SKID-MARKS GUY (proper n.): a guy who leaves signs in his underwear; i.e., Mr. Steve Brady

STRAIGHT-GAY MAN (n., plentiful in New York): a gay guy who plays sports and won't fuck you (see also "gay-straight man")

SURPRISE FIX-UP (n.): when two married friends have a single male friend "fake" coming into a restaurant while you're eating with them, to fix the two of you up; very annoying

T

TARTINI (n., delicious): cranberry-flavored vodka

THIRD-DATE QUESTION (n.): "When was your last serious relationship?"

TWO-BLOW-JOB CHICK (proper n.): a girl who puts blow jobs in the coming attractions that the guy's never going to see in the actual movie

U

UPSEX (v.): to trump a friend who has really big sex news by revealing even bigger sex news

UP-THE-BUTT GIRL (n.): 1) the girl you become when you let a guy go there; 2) the girl men won't marry

URBAN RELATIONSHIP MYTH (n.): an unbelievable fairy tale concocted by women to make their love lives seem less hopeless, except it makes you feel even more hopeless because this fabulous, magical relationship is never happening to you; usually involves rain

USED-DATE PARTY (n.): a party where one brings a person they are no longer interested in

V

VAGUE GESTURE (abstract n.): a hard-to-read possible gesture of affection, such as a dozen birthday roses with the card, "Best Wishes"

W

WALK OF SHAME (n.): the morning-after walk home from a hot date, when you're still wearing the outfit that enabled you to spend the night

WOODY AND MIA [*sic*] (abstract n.): what single men yearn for; a kind of separate togetherness that involves two people being together when they want to be and apart when they want to be

Y

YOGASM (n.): an orgasm brought on by postyoga sex with someone in your class; sex that is deemed necessary after a sad attempt at tantric celibacy

SARAH JESSICA PARKER:

I like to think our crew is different from others. We have the best people, and the majority of our crew has been with us since 1997, which is very unusual. We are very attached to one another and care very deeply about each other. I've never in my whole working life had an experience where I felt that. Sometimes it's the crew who I show up for on days when I am really tired. I feel like I perform for them. When I know one of them is going to be gone the next day, it makes my stomach hurt. They work such hideous hours, and we just try to remind them how much we appreciate them. It's undoable without this crew. They are all incredibly bright, incredibly interesting, and it doesn't hurt that the men are all very *handsome.*

This book was produced by *Melcher Media* Inc.,
55 Vandam Street, New York, NY 10013.

PUBLISHER . . . . Charles Melcher

EDITOR . . . . Lia Ronnen

PRODUCTION DIRECTOR . . . . Andrea Hirsh

WRITER . . . . Amy Sohn

ART DIRECTION AND DESIGN . . . . Number Seventeen

Special Thanks
Sarah Jessica Parker
Amy B. Harris
Cindy Chupack
and everyone at *Sex and the City* and HBO
who has participated in and given their time for this book.

Thanks
Andrew Ackermann, Royce Bergman, Craig Blankenhorn, Duncan Bock, Louise Burke, Tom Bozzelli, Kim Cattrall, Sarah Condon, Bree Conover, Jeremy Conway, Eric Cyphers, Martha Crawford, Kristin Davis, Jason De Bari, Martin Felli, Patricia Field, Sarah Glasser, Daniel Greenberg, Cristina Greeven, Michael Patrick King, Jessica Marshall, Pete Megler, Gordon McGregor, Lauren McKenna, John Melfi, John Meils, Michelle Morris, Allison Murray, Grace Naughton, Cynthia Nixon, Richard Oren, Jeff Peters, Jane Raab, Molly Rogers, Candace Ross, Buster Scher, Russell Schwartz, Darren Star, Liate Stehlik, Carolyn Strauss, Angela Tarantino, Marian Toy, Marie Walker, Megan Worman, and everyone at Number Seventeen: Eva Hueckmann, Nomi Joy, Emily Oberman, and Bonnie Siegler.

About the Contributors

AMY SOHN
is the author of the novel *Run Catch Kiss* (Simon & Schuster) and
the *New York* magazine column, "Naked City." Her second novel, *My Old Man,*
will be published by Simon & Schuster in 2004. She lives in Brooklyn.

MELCHER MEDIA
is an award-winning book producer based in New York City.

NUMBER SEVENTEEN
is a New York based, award-winning, multi-disciplinary design firm
working in print, film, and television.

Photography Credits

All photographs: Craig Blankenhorn/HBO except for the following:
page 6: courtesy, Sarah Jessica Parker; pages 8-9, 14-15, 16-17: HBO; pages 38-39, photographs of Cindy Chupack and Jenny Bicks, courtesy Cindy Chupack; page 41-43, childhood photos courtesy, Kristin Davis; page 62, all photos of Carrie's apartment: Richard Felber; except photo of Aidan's chair, photo of bookshelf with personal pictures, and Carrie's living room: Craig Blankenhorn/HBO; page 67, purse and shoe: HBO; pages 68-69, continuity and bag photos: HBO; pages 80-81: HBO; page 82, childhood photos, courtesy, Cynthia Nixon; page 84, bottom right of Cynthia Nixon, courtesy, Sarah Jessica Parker; page 100, top photo courtesy, James Hoff; photo of John Melfi courtesy, Joe Collins; page 101, photos of writing team and Jennifer McNamara, courtesy, Amy B. Harris; photo of Michael Patrick King with cow, courtesy James Hoff; page 102, photo of Chris Noth with make-up, courtesy Sarah Jessica Parker; photo of stand-ins, courtesy, James Hoff; page 103, photos of Antonia Ellis and Michael Berenbaum, courtesy Amy B. Harris; photo of Wendey Stanzler, courtesy Wendey Stanzler; pages 107-109, childhood photos, courtesy, Kim Cattrall; page 116, high-school photo of Chris Noth, courtesy, Chris Noth; page 120, photo of John Corbett with Sarah Jessica in pearls, courtesy, Sarah Jessica Parker; pages 124-125: childhood photos courtesy, David Eigenberg; pages 128-129, childhood photos, courtesy Willie Garson; page 135: Charlotte as a man: HBO; pages 158-159, all photos courtesy, Sarah Jessica Parker except group photo courtesy John Melfi, photos of Amy Harris, Cindy Chupack, Angela Tarantino and Grace Naughton: Condé Nast Publications; photo of Sarah Jessica in blue dress with three men in top right, courtesy, Amy B. Harris.